Ever wondered why your visualisations aren't working so well.

Improve your success rate now.

REALITY DOESN'T EXIST

The Missing Bit to the Law of Abundance

Both a Memoir and an Exploration of Positive Thinking

This book will make you think

Written by an aging Irish psychic

R. ADAMS

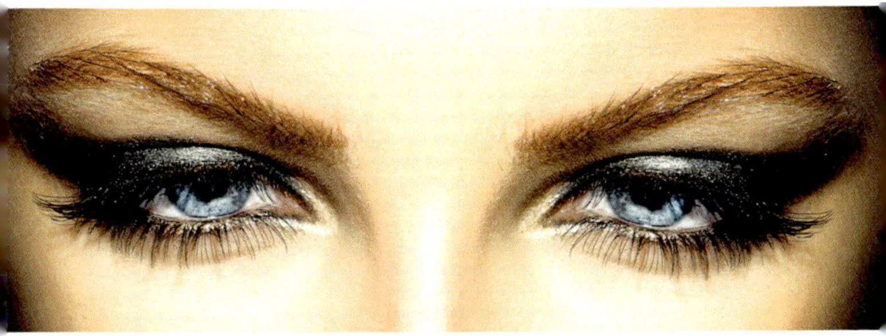

REALITY DOESN'T EXIST – AMAZON

£1~~1~~2.99

chartexcell@gmail.com

Rosemary Adams

14 Hazelbrook Ave. Bangor

N. Ireland BT20 3HZ

Frontespiece

"Write your story as it needs to be written. Write it honestly, and tell it as best you can. I'm not sure that there are any other rules. Not ones that matter."

\- *Neil Gaiman*

Aged 20/21

This book is dedicated to my brother Stuart who in his own way lives a spiritual life in his garden

Thank you for coming along with me this far

and to Beryl Crawford, whom I miss

With thanks to Gerry Miller, Bangor and
Canon Ronnie Nesbitt,
Bangor Abbey and Coleraine

For their help and support

REALITY DOESN'T EXIST

The missing bit to the Law of Abundance

By

R. Adams

INDEX

Introduction

Who is the Author?

It's when I look up through a Perspex glass ceiling covering an outside beer garden that I see a high sky covered with white clouds moving fast It's an Atlantic sky and I see again Donegal and Dalyan, which is a name I give to certain places. These are old Victorian stone alleyways, black stone, covered in ivy and up the steep stone steps you can look back at surf rising through terraced houses, either in your mind in memory or in actual life if you happen to be there. The back ground land rises sharply and hasn't changed in 100 years. Wild flowers grow high, an open loose yellow they are quite big on six foot stems, reaching upwards. I haven't seen them before. You can guess I'm rooted in place.

My place is the North West, but I've travelled. I return back here in later life as swallows do, this time not to leave again, it is inbred, I am part of it and have been all my life. It was troubling to leave. I am marked by place, some events and a spiritual urge. I am a child of civil insurrection and of the Sixties. So, I'm old you guess and now I would have to agree. I look in the mirror and I have aged. It happened slowly. There is a phrase I've heard that bankruptcy happens slowly then quickly and age is much the same. It suddenly comes upon you but not all at once. While my horizons, once wide, stay open, my ability to get there narrows. My name is Rosemary and I'm not well known. I have travelled a spiritual path all my life.

And I have come up with answers that satisfy me, in so far as they go, after searches and thought I have arrived at these conclusions and I would like to share them with you, as I think they may help. To get the best from these you may need to stay focused and be prepared to leave some well accepted shibboleths at the kitchen door, which is where they really belong.

Times may or may not be changing. Many times over many years people have thought they were on the threshold of discovery, and sometimes they were, and then years later their freshnesses and original thought in their time too became passe's and another generation believed, look we are on the threshold of something, It is common now to see these times as a time of spiritual awakening, a time when people everywhere realise that they too are gods, and that may be the case. If all comes to naught it will be a pity, but not unknown in history. Good causes do at times come to naught. We tend to be indoctrinated in the successful ones. We'll see, I suppose, and this book should help. That's my thought and my focus and my reason for writing.

I am writing from my own experience. The things I have seen and lived through form the basis to this book, and not just my awareness culled from other writers, whom I am most grateful to as they have helped alter my view of my world very positively. Nonetheless, it is my own experience that forms my beliefs in another reality and I know both my thoughts and my experience can revolutionise yours. How happy an occurrence would that be, to influence the world or have my words like seeds fall on unfertile ground, another possible outcome. It is up to me and up to you, how I write, how you perceive. I know you will give me a chance by reading on and you will benefit from all the events and conclusions outlined in the coming pages. Even if only to become more curious and question the "world as a reality" that you see around you.

We live together in a world that is not what it appears to be. There are groupings and there are interests and there are those who protect the interests they hold or believe to be right. I have no rights to offer, there's no one way of viewing our world, but I have a clearer view than many and that view or belief structure is outlined in this book, in the belief it will help you live out your life with clarity and support, for there is much support, just as there may at times be opposition. So enjoy all coming pages, all the ups and downs, for there were a few, just as there will have been for you. We get where we're going through exploration and an open mind. We experience the same things and the same opportunities lie open for all of us.

1. You are Supreme Spiritual Beings

I am a trained astrologer and if this turns you off, so be it. It's inherent, like other skills, and now it is a support. It is an intensely spiritual discipline, you will find few astrologers, if any at all, without faith in spirit, in a world that is intensely greater than the one we see. You can call us charlatans, some scientists do, but there is a wealth of training behind what we do and a wealth of knowledge. It has given me a certainty, above and beyond what I might otherwise have achieved, and I would not wish to live life without it. It gives a perspective that other disciplines don't quite reach, it vastly outstrips psychology, yet psychology is it.

I mention this in passing for the moment but will return later to look at it in greater detail.

What I believe and am now teaching comes from my life experiences and insights into this and other pathways to God. In my father's house there are many mansions and there are many pathways but I cannot think of a better pathway than astrology as it encompasses so much, and it requires no ritual. It contains no candles or chanting.

If you follow a religious path, I will try to wean you away from that slightly. There is nothing wrong with the core concept of most religions, but there can be with the practice. You already know this and perhaps let that awareness go at times for you would have to be blind not to see what lies around you. Many religions seek devotees, believers, followers, cash. You are supreme spiritual beings, do you really want to be a follower?

How is your life? How goes it with you? Are you mired in debt, up to your thighs in sexual affairs, driven by odd compulsions, afraid to think of death, gripped by daily political change, raging against the dying of the light, living with painful illness, content but afraid to think, closing off certain areas of life as they are too difficult to deal with, afraid of change? We have lots of issues and many of them can alter with a change of approach. This may be called belief.

And I call upon you to have belief as you are so much greater than you may believe.

I am Cardinal, I take action. If something displeases, I'm off, and at the same time I find it hard to let go of people and places. I hold them with me as a shield against unfamiliar pathways and the immense effort of starting again. They nourish me. They have mattered and, therefore they still do. Even if they're elsewhere, dead or not in touch to me they are part of my life. There were many met *en route* for longer or lesser times, who touched fleetingly or intensely and they form part of what upheld or formed me. They have informed me. They've made me what I am and what I'm not. Their memory walks with me. We meet again those we agree to meet. Nothing is lost.

2. Place and Spiritual Background

If we start with civil insurrection, I grew up in Derry in the Sixties. Well, more appropriately the Fifties, but in general those early years passed without travail. The troubles started in earnest in my late teens, though I saw sandbags in areas of town when I was twelve or so. We didn't much take them seriously because people never think their world is about to be profoundly altered. I had a year when I stayed in the street playing locally with friends and didn't study much What benign God looked down on that year and said have some fun, child. I still remember it as a golden time. I think we all have years like that, when things swim easily along and the sun shines benignly on every place in the known world. Years after the fun year I became Deputy to the Head Girl, probably because there was no way on earth I wanted to be Head Girl. It suited me, a title and not much work. I did and do work but the year of joyful living in my home street with my occasional friends remains with me as a happy experience.

The spiritual side was always there. I saw faces in the dark at night, I dreamed of seances, mediumship, extrasensory abilities. I needed to be special. In the way of mysticism, I picked up a lot and said little. My membranes were leaky. If you imagined them as a frontier every would-be invader would get through. I had no barrier against the outside world in all its nuances. I picked them all up and longed to be a psychiatrist. There was one on TV in the Sixties, where the psychiatrist had time to visit people's homes and inspect their family set-up and explain it as the fundamental cause to crises. In present day terms the show was utterly unlikely. It was slowly paced with no urgency. A fan shaped light over a Harley Street entrance at the end of every show drew me in and welcomed in the night. I longed to be part of that cosy life. In personality terms the actor was a close mirror image of myself, he matched in pattern and intent and that may why I identified with it. I watch it again now with liking, though society has changed and the stories are outdated. It retains its ability to captivate its past audience.

I give you this background information so that you will have some idea of who the writer is, because, well, it's obvious isn't it? The more familiarity, the greater the chance of getting through. I find, as I get older, that I come closer to what I started out as. Do you? There's a peace to be had in old places. Slowly we return to our roots and wonder why we spent so much time and effort outliving them. I've learned things along the way and I wish to share them with you. You should enjoy this and get something out of it. That may be what spirit said as it sent us down the birth canal – I hope you enjoy the trip, it won't take long and we'll have you back before you know it. Spirit can have a bad sense of humour.

3. How to Access Your Hidden Spirit Guides.

It pains me to say this, but we do have them. I'm happier with them now than initially. They went a little against my previous thinking. I now hear from them and appreciate their words. They speak in short phrases, but the gist is clear. Foolish woman, when I continue on something they'd rather not see, you have no idea, when I've avoided doing something they've pressured about. They're laconic, and not humorous and they do not cosset. It's not like being wrapped in warm cotton wool, it's more like being trained because they do want to pursue the best. I take what they say and try to adapt to it, it is so, so much easier to go with them, because they tend to persist.

Maybe you don't believe they exist or you see them as angels and it is possible we encounter spirit in the way best suited to us and a different approach may work best for you, and you and you. This book aims to help you contact your inner wisdom, with the understanding that it is not all and only you. There is a spiritual realm that tries always to come through, using nudges, hints and at times direct instruction. It may be difficult for you to believe in, especially when times are difficult and you need support the most.

We get support from spirit. You may not yet hear from spirit direct, but there is another valid way of getting support.

We all have an inner guide and we contain within us the answer to many questions. We often drown this guide out with everyday things, drinks or drugs being one way, busyness another. We all have that voice. Sometimes we follow on, sometimes we don't. Even when we see a sign in the street saying life is about to change, how could that possibly be for us? Who are we that life should speak to us in this way? Who are we?

We are a part of spirit. We're here to achieve something, to experience things, pleasures and difficulties that make us question some of our life decisions and perhaps do things differently. As I've said, we drown this out in a million ways. We overeat, we over-sex, we over-media, we buy things, we become ill, we concentrate on anything but spirit. We refuse to listen and we do this because at times it seems difficult to follow spirit as our life may seem all right, not wonderful, but not worth disturbing. We're mired in the mud but we don't realise it or we pretend it isn't there and mud can stick a lot. We get bogged down and it seems only the brave and courageous manage to raise their heads above the average, so it seems, but it's not really true. We can all do it, all it needs is a little intent.

Suggestion number one here

I was going to call this rule number one, but no, just no. I believe so little in rules. This is it. Believe you can get somewhere and keep at it. If you want to progress in understanding life and why you are here, you have to make it a lifetime's work. It's the same with any intention. You'll get derailed, but it pays to persevere. Keep reading, keep praying, and begin – if you haven't already – to meditate. In all the daily busyness that occurs as above, spirit gets drowned out. Meditation is nothing other than pausing the mental process, slowing things down so that your heartbeat slows a little and your active mind relaxes. It relaxes enough to let messages through from your inner knowing and from spirit which is an outer knowing. I do not know how advanced spirit is. It seems to me, from various experiences, that spirit is multi-dimensional, that there are different levels and you can't be sure what level things are coming from. I mean positive levels here. To my surprise, I no longer think of spirit as just an overriding entity or ethereal energy, though it is that. I think there are beings there too with their different levels of knowing or becoming. It's not a conclusion I sought – I'd prefer to think of one amorphous and all-knowing mass – but at this point in my life I think we're dealing with levels of spirit. This need not concern you too much – just be alert to anything that comes through. If you have an urgent need to take action or change things, look at your usual responses. You may have a character that throws things overboard in favour of the new. If that is the case, and your inner responses say to rush, then hold hard for a while in a meditative, or thoughtful, state. Think about whether you're following an outdated pattern in your rush for the new and if, in a calm and meditative state of mind, you reach the decision that change is, in whatever position you are in, desirable, then take what action you can and try, always, to take the other person into account. Do no harm. Do what you will and harm none. Those are well-known words from the witchy world, but still sensible. Still unsure how to meditate? Find somewhere quiet, away from interruption, make yourself comfortable – sitting upright or inclined, best not to lie down as you might go to sleep – quiet your mind and just sit. Peace will come and with it some understanding of things that might benefit you to understand. Keep at it week after week, for just as you do leg exercises or facial tapping, it's the repetition that gets you somewhere. You can oom and uum as you like, as sound is said to hold a vibration, but there's no need. You can just sit and if there are days or weeks where you haven't time or can't be bothered, do not concern yourself unduly. Life is fairly long and even a 2/3 success rate will get you quite far along your path in terms of altering perspective for the better. Meditation is a wondrous calming thing to do. It slows you right down and you may find that life's solutions speed right up. Things become simpler, so do try it.

4. Systems for Accessing Spirit

Do not bother unduly with how you do it. You'll find a lot of techniques, Buddhist chanting, Hindu yogic poses, Western autogenic training, intentional soundbites repeated, listening to meditative tapes, so many systems. But that is all they are truly – systems that suit the peoples they originated from. They may or may not work. They are systems of behaviour that spread and grow in acceptance from time to time. Use them or not. All you really need to do is try to switch off, to experience calm and to feel any hints or new requirements that might be coming through to you. Don't even worry about remembering these. Your body will recall what was linked to this deeper peace and you will remember, without really thinking. The ego and intellect are superbright, but what you need, truly, is a connection to the inner, the knowing part of yourself and thereby find a connection to the divine, that is both within and without yourselves. Then pay caring attention to your environment and take action calmly, knowing that it is better to take action than to sit in torment, for we do, don't we?

Pray and this is slightly different to meditation, for here we are talking to someone and asking for help or understanding. With all due reverence, pray and thank them daily for what they are doing, for you do not know what they are doing for you, but you can be fairly confident that somewhere someone is listening and they are on your side. It doesn't much matter what you've done – which is probably not much in the bad scheme of things if you're into reading books – you can start again. It may not be possible to undo poor actions, but you can aim for better actions at present and that present will spread out and affect your future and the future of those around you. Pray, and know and expect to be listened to. Pray and know too that somewhere the results of your prayer may to a degree be changing the past, people at a remove may feel your intent without being aware of it. It's like absent healing. So the past can change slightly, but effectively we are concerned with the present – and, of course, your upcoming eternal life, but you're not there yet so focus on the present. It's the best you can do. You are cared for and you are supported and sometimes your worst enemy is yourself. That's if you raise your vibrations. If your vibrations are still on the low side, your worst enemy may indeed be other people. *L'enfer c'est les autres*. They surely can bite. Raise your vibrations. Fly above their heads.

5. Jumping into Rivers

All good seminars I've attended, and there are many, have started with the speaker informing us a little of his or her life, what happened in their past to push them onto a spiritual or developmental path. They overlap but they're not always the same. So I thought I'd give you the same, some insight into what has happened in my own life to make me think I could illuminate something or anything in a multi-layered spiritual universe, for that is what we are in.

Leaving out the early years, I jumped into a river in my forties but it took a while to reach that stage. It took many years of seeking. I jumped in following instructions, it took guts but by that stage I'd been living with paranoid psychosis for many years, hearing voices and facing terrors. I was used to courage. I floated for a while and looked at the sky. It was very calm, the river was smooth and I wanted to stay there. Maybe I should have floated for longer, but I started to "take action", which was maybe not right in that case for I was truly at peace and had no wish to disrupt that. I started to swim but didn't get very far with it. The reason for which, because I'm an average swimmer, was that I didn't have to. Unexpectedly, in an instant, I found myself out of the water and on a beam. To underline the point, one minute

I was in the water, the next minute I was out. Dripping, wet, very heavy and standing on a beam looking down the river and seeing - no-one. Up above on the wharf there were people, but where I stood, not a one.

In many ways later this haunted me, for we choose our response. I saw the miracle, I was blown away, but I also rued the fact that I was unable to replicate it. I tried once again but not sufficiently and I should have tried a third time, but didn't. Foolish woman. The second jump later brought trauma. I was rescued, but traumatised to the point where I think I remained unconscious for a long period of time. When I did wake I found a group of concerned consultants over me. They vanished once I opened my eyes and they tell you nothing. No-one says anything. No-one ever does. Nurses see spirit leaving a body and maybe later report to a newspaper. If it's out of the ordinary, believe me, people rationalise to a large degree.

After two attempts I couldn't bring myself to try again. My reason was that I didn't want to end up in hospital again but that's a pretty meagre excuse. I regret it and yet I know in the same situation, at the same time, I would almost certainly do the same thing. I ran out of puff. The medical profession will tell you what I lived through was impossible, and therefore didn't exist. But spirit cannot be weighed or measured. It is intangible. It is light, it is air, it is fire, it is instinct and it exists.

I jumped, I flew, I had spent fourteen years praying to spirit every minute of every day, I wanted to progress. I just got so far.

6. Pay no Attention

So there I was, in severe regret about not having gone further. Yet I had gone somewhere and that is what propels me to write this book. But in the knowledgc that my experience of spirit may reach a broader audience. I write to entertain and to inform, I'm a reasonable writer. I write because I have no other way of saying, once again, what I most heartily know, that spirit exists all around us, that it is sentient, that it hears, that it wishes us well but is still somewhat detached and that it may, at times of crisis, take action to protect or to inform. It is simply greater than we, yet we are part of it and it is inherent in us, in all of us, no matter our deeds and no matter our beliefs, it is within and without us and it would prefer that we were with it. So much of our modern life mitigates against this. We have no time and that is our choice. It is also thrust upon us by a technical society that wishes, at some level, to reduce us all to an unthinking mass, a populace than can be advertised to, instructed, brainwashed. We go along so easily and spend waking hours watching, listening, absorbing everything that is oh so very, very wrong. It is possible that it suits many vested interests that we remain so, unthinking, incapable, unaware of all that dwells within us each.

Unaware too of our personal potential, which is and always has been vast.

Suggestion number two

Pay little attention to what they tell you in the media. Inform yourselves about what appears to be going on, the *menu du jour* in the world, then switch off. It can only make you sadder or angrier, it certainly won't make you wiser and it does what it is intended to do. It makes you poorer.

7. Past Lives Perhaps

Spirit and awareness of spirit may be different for everyone. I have no way of knowing, I am only one person with one person's awareness, but I am a very old person. I've lived before and I meet this at times in place. I said earlier I am a person of place, place informs me and reaches out to tell me I have been there before, I have a connection to place. You may feel this too, it is hugely reassuring, to enter a foreign realm and know something of where you have been before. A singer in an American casino, a seaman walking down from the hills, both dying young and both without leaving children behind. Something I will do in this lifetime – no descendants and no regret as I have no need to reproduce. I will, after all, be back. That's the essential ego trip, isn't it, reproducing yourself?

And I have no need now to look further at these lives. They are gone or they are a product of my imagination, depending on how you understand them, linked to some issue that needs to be resolved or understood further in this life. No matter, I go there sometimes because these are places I loved and felt comfortable in and places I felt, as a child, that I would like to visit. I longed to go to America. I looked at calendars with pictures sent from there. I had a pen pal in North Africa. He sent me photographs of Morocco. Things reproduce and we may indeed meet the same sort of experience from one time to another. What is sure is that in this one life we meet the same sort of experience until we gain some understanding about it. That is psychology, not necessarily spirituality, and the events themselves are not inherently important. If we experience difficulty it may teach us something but it may not be at all necessary. We can rise above it, for most of us, though, that takes years of practice and quite possibly years of trouble. How we vex our lives by expecting trouble. How we analyse and try and how we focus on woe and what we focus on grows.

When we look at the ocean, it swells and ebbs and flows and shines in the evening light like diamonds and we lose ourselves for a while in contemplation of the wildness, the savagery, the calm, the jellyfish, the delicate details of shells, little homes abandoned by some creature on the shore edge and we know, for that time, that we are linked, that we are connected and we are nourished. Let's try for nourishment for out of that our spiritual connection grows stronger and we are replenished, we are renewed and if we live in a desert area, we look at cacti and barren hills and feel connected to native energies that are different to western ones but still connected to all that is. We feel part of our environment and here too we are nourished. For all of us there is a connection that is old, it is part of what we used to be. We long to be reconnected to it and modern life does everything it can to remove us ever further from it.

8. Belief Systems

I grew up with religion, most of us do. It was all around. It seeped from images of the Virgin, from communion dresses, from catechisms and it was alluring. It spoke of realms that were fantastical, every bit as enchanting as Santa Claus. And that is what religion is, a myth, a comforting interpretation of where we are, a call to battle, an urge to belong, an urge especially to obey. We are born into it and educated into it and no-one tells us that it is mythic, no-one has the nous to say to us when we are a little older that it is an uplifting story intended to support us, for it is also intended to keep us in line and it is indeed possible that these older people who could or should lift the mists a little for us as we grow cannot do so as they have never dared clear the mists for themselves. Social engineering can be a powerful force even in areas of the world where it is not also accompanied by violence. We attach to our imposed belief structures like limpets to rocks and we are often so mistaken.

What is not in doubt is that our belief structures, even where wrong, can uphold us through times of trouble. We cling to them and they may very well bring us through. When they don't we rail against heaven or we despair or we reinforce our beliefs even further.

When prophecy fails can also be a powerful force in upholding our beliefs, as we fall back on our failed beliefs even more in the knowledge that next time they will definitely work and where would we be without them, a bit like gambling. Sometimes this approach works, but it may be better to look and think elsewhere.

There are various studies that have looked at this patterning, I won't repeat them here.

I cannot advise against belief structures as I do think that any belief is better than none. If we truly believe that prayer can help, then it does and it will. If we believe in spirit, spirit helps, if we place our trust in four leafed shamrocks, they too may help. Any belief that we are supported will help. It is our belief that works miracles, not the thing we believe in, although in these previous examples there is a difference. Both spirit and four leafed shamrocks exist. You can connect with either. But only spirit will actively connect back. I think that four leafed shamrocks are not sentient to any great degree, although if you connect them up to an electrode and threaten them with cutting, they may react. A protective sort of reaction. They are unlikely to reach out to help you achieve your goals or feel more at peace in the way that spirit does and will.

Connect to spirit if you can and forget about the niceties of your particular religion. These niceties are only scaffolding that's been put there over centuries to help you believe. They have no reality in or of themselves.

Look at how religions evolve over centuries from their original position of love. They become complex and separate. In backward areas they create division, war, entrenched ideas, which have little to do with their original purpose which lay in the teaching, normally by one enlightened person, then spreading through believers until they became vaster and under the aegis of "authority". That's when they tend to go wrong.

Better, I think, to trust in spirit directly as we are all sparks of the divine, all interlinked, even though we might appear to be independent of one another, we are vastly dependent.

9. The Study Stage of Life

So what happened to make me think I could gainfully tell you about my life in expectation that it may make some positive difference to your own – for that is what we are here for, is it not? No reader is really too concerned about my ups and downs but you almost all will hope that any experiences I tell you about might help you better understand your own successes or failures, not that anything is ever really failed, as we learn from all we do, but sometimes we don't do – well, quite as well as we should, do we? This relates to me as much as to you.

Until thirty I was more or less contained. I fitted in and I did, fit in. I had a good social life. I liked learning and I inhabited places of learning for quite a few years and would love to go back. There is nothing so cosseting as the lecture round and nothing much to worry about except how far your money might go in the food direction. Drinks were, at that time, generally paid for elsewhere. That was the norm. We were lucky with our generation.

At around thirty I started to change. For a start I left a not very well paid job and took a year off – remember that this was forty years ago and not so common. I'd had enough and thought I could make it independently, self-employed in a variety of directions, which I subsequently did after struggles, moves and continued effort. Earning much less than if I'd stayed employed, but with a wealth of experience and quite a degree of self-worth. It wasn't usual for a woman at that time to do this, but it evolved and I moved with it. I was fairly tired taking instruction from, on the whole, quite pleasant hierarchies. That was also when I relaxed my idea of what people would say and sought out a class in what I was most interested in – astrology. I'm not going there yet but it was an ever present and absorbing interest. I met a range of very interesting people and started studies that would continue for many years. I'm a writer, so I wrote – articles, horoscopes, personal charts, all of this alongside my day interest in language, so it was a mix and that's what I did to earn money. Money wasn't plentiful, but what I did do seemed worthwhile in the large scheme of life where it's better to do what excites you than to clock in for the day, bored out of your wits, with office romances and scapes and struggles and gossip. That seems fine when you're immersed in it, but are you truly getting far?

You may want to ask yourself this question. Am I getting very far? Is there anything else I could do that would be way more enjoyable?

Many get rich quick writers suggest starting a business of you own is the best option for getting ahead and I can't disagree. Continuing to work as before, I became immersed in spiritual studies, because there were so many options to look at and several book shops specialising in the esoteric. Not witchcraft, or the dark end of things, as I never could see the positivity in having a skull sitting on your desk, rather positive thinking, channelling which was popular at the time, past life experience, energy massage, so alongside intense studies I spent my spare time involved in a lot. And I rather regret not getting even more immersed, but I always hung back a little, not wanting to put all my eggs in one basket. I suppose the basket I was really involved in was language, foreign words and how to interpret them in a way that I would be more than satisfied with. I was happy with my choice and remain so. I made enough to live on and I was successful.

10. Distraction.

I wrote this book in order that you and I might achieve something of worth in the world in which we presently live. This is a world of stimuli, where we are bombarded by sound. All around us is distraction and we can live distraction our entire life. This is ultimately dissatisfying and to drown out this realisation, which is perhaps disquieting, we seek and find further distraction. Line it up for ourselves, from emotional to physical, intelligent to positively dim ways of being, we live our lives in various ways in order to avoid looking at it. We cling to distraction all the more when we feel ourselves drowning in it. It is not nice to drown, we feel, so we grasp at the nearest raft, which is all too often ... another distraction. Distraction should be a fleeting thing, a moment's joy or respite, but our raft often becomes our life and we cling to it against the sensation of drowning, so we drown even more.

This is life in the western world and although there are murmurs which move against the stream, the present stream is, in the main, one of distraction. When I die I would like to think I'd done something good in life, altered something that needed changing, left something behind. The time of gurus is past. We only need gurus to hold a pointer to the road to follow. We leave them behind, if we're wise. It is time to abandon our idols, it is time to go within.

11. Decisions to Change.

Do you do what you don't want to? Do you people please? Are you weighed down by family responsibility? Are you concerned, caring, worn out at day end? You may be doing yourself a disservice, and no matter how urgent, how time pressed, there is always, always a way of saying no and doing less. It is resolutely up to you.

When you make a decision to change, to dress in a way that suits you, to alter your time constraints to do less, to read something that others consider outlandish, to tell someone close to you that they have truly offended, to stand up for yourself, that is when life will start to move and, as they tell you in books, all that is nasty will come to the surface. Sometimes, as in life generally, there are vested interests and people, unless challenged, can be selfish. If you yourself are guilty of demanding of others, just stop and do something for yourself for once. They're not there to serve, they're not there to rescue, they're there to love and be loved, but of course daily social intercourse runs along different routes and the love gets buried deep. If you're hitting your head against a brick wall caused by daily circumstance or addiction, stop, pause, pray and try to alter what you so wrongly believe cannot be changed. It's all nothingness, and nothingness can take whatever shape we want it to. So want better, desire better, go for better – at the very least, go for change. And if they challenge you, as they might, pay them no mind. Pleasantly, for after all they too have their own conditioning and their own voices in their past telling them what to think, what to do, how to react. How to blend in. Try not to, aim for standing out, in all your glory, I won't call it uniqueness, for we are all, in our hopes and desires, really very similar. Choose what is good about yourself, choose your own interests, and follow up, enhance, enjoy, make time and see where it goes. Every small step matters and if that's all you think you can achieve – well, you're mistaken.

12. The Light of Spirit

When I look at the Wild Atlantic Way I see spirit. I see light dancing on waves and brightness shining through on even the dullest day and I see my parents and grandparents and people in my past life standing on the far Donegal shore and I relive the days from my youth. These where days when we would travel into Inishowen, Island of Eoghain, who in turn was son of a High King of Ireland, but we didn't know much of that at the time. We would sit on a tartan rug and eat damp sandwiches. My elderly grandmothers would sit in deckchairs and enjoy their day out. These were days when the light at the end of the day spoke of eternity and vast spaces, when the golden light of evening would shine through an arch from Shipquay Street into the Guildhall and when peace and tranquillity and heavenly space seemed to join in a fusion that is quintessential to the North West and to my life. We all have days like that. I lived with spirit in those times and was aware of it as a feeling of possibility, connection, tranquillity. The evening light at that time of day came as a benediction and a hand beckoning forward. The world in that place at that time was filled with potential, and potential was spiritual, ineffable, unknowable but tangible for a few hours at evening at the end of the known world, which is where I grew up.

I grew up at the end of the known world.

So I thought a lot.

13. Schopenhauer and Aloneness

Schopenhauer said *"to live alone is the fate of great souls".* Schopenhauer was a German philosopher from the C19th, and the internet is up to scratch here in a way that I am not. It's easy to lift a quote without knowing where it came from. It appears that he said this. That is reassuring as to paraphrase another great, namely Shirley Conran who was influential in the 70s and who I am more informed about than Schopenhauer, life is too short to well, study philosophers in depth, especially at this stage of life, so I'll happily refer to the internet. I can't claim total ignorance, but close to total would not be far off. There may be a lot to this quote, which is why I mention it. Solitude may be important in the way of things. Think of images of gurus, sitting cross-legged on a mountain top, alone. Think of important spiritual figures leading ashrams also alone in the midst of admirers. To live a spiritual life is to go within. We can't easily do that if we're bombarded with media, noise, or spousal demands. We need to take time here, carve out hours for ourselves. Some prefer to spend a great deal of time alone and some have aloneness thrust upon them, drawn by something in their own personal nature or events in their earlier lives. It's at times when you've given up attachment to other things that spirit can be heard most clearly, it speaks quietly within and guides gently at all times. Spirit is always with us, but we hear it best at rest, when we are perhaps alone.

Another suggestion here

Carve out space for yourself, even if you have to insist, relax, go within and know that spirit does come through – if not now, eventually. How will you know? You will hear it.

Solitude makes introspection easier, and we do need time to think. This is different to meditation, in that you may when alone be thinking deeply, and both have effect. Contemplation of life or ideas takes time, ideas may come out of the blue in the middle of action, but they may result from prior introspection and willingness to hear. Because they are always speaking.

How do I know this? I have for long periods of time heard from spirit. It speaks as words in my mind and is not always admiring. I have not known spirit to criticise, but it can be detached, stating a view in a matter of fact way. "Foolish woman". It comes through most easily early in the morning, and I know what they refer to and, if I tell you confidentially, it is, just between us, that I have not gone far enough spiritually. And I know to what that refers and they are correct. But I also know, as do they, that I have come far from where I started and where I started was not that bad. I started with a mystical view of life and I followed that. I sought to become closer to God, and in that I have been successful. So I have come far and I want to share what I have learned and my view of life with you, as it has brought me awareness, peacefulness, a sense of achievement and a knowledge that at all times, in all situations, there is a spiritual life around us which supports, nourishes and informs. It is up to us to listen to it. There is no obligation but the outcome is advantageous. And the ground on which you stand will be firm. It will no longer waiver when assailed. You, my friend, are strong and stronger than you think. In whatever place you find yourself, know that going within is the way forward. And if you are surrounded by demand, noise, others? Buy yourself a shed. Go within.

14. When Others Attack

Sometimes, en route to greatness or even an upswing in fortune, you will trigger a few buttons. People are slow to change. Mockery can be the go-to for unintelligent people who feel threatened. Who are you to say or do that? It's unfortunate but it happens and it can stop you from following paths that might bring you where you long to go. If you're truly wonderful on creating positivity in life, it shouldn't, but on the way to drawing to you what you want, it might.

Try not to let it get to you for that is what it's intended to do.

Also don't expect it, for then it will certainly appear. Do what you do, change as you can, if you're destined for greatness keep going because as spiritual beings that's what we all can achieve. Yes, all of us. Even those you think shouldn't.

And here I am being all too human. You'll have to excuse me. Now, where's my dagger?

In my Thirties

15. Grace

Keeping you up-to-date here with my life's photos. Let's continue with Schopenhauer as no good research should go to waste, especially at this stage of life, and besides, it's interesting. He adopted the world-as-appearance school of thought. Accordingly we experience things around us as representation that is we see things as dependent on ourselves as viewers and not as a world that necessarily exists of itself.

I have every reason to support this idea, it's essentially what I'm trying to get across in this book, so maybe others have got there before me, but maybe too you'll find me more accessible than Schopenhauer or other philosophers. I'm talking from personal experience, and although I'm altogether interested in theory and could spend much time in debate, I'm speaking here from experience, many years of experience and it's something I think is vital you should take on board. The world as we see it is not there. It's dependent on us as viewers. This may blow your mind, but it's not original. I remember as a child hearing the debate that if there was no-one in the forest would there be a sound of a tree falling, that sort of thing. The forest is there, but only because we agree it to be so, only because that's what we expect to see.

What if we change our expectations? This is what lies at the basis to positive thinking. If we can think a thing differently, it may turn out to be so. There are many books written about positive thinking and it's a discipline which works quite often and sometimes doesn't. It depends on our belief system, the degree to which we can persuade our inner self that we are worthy of what we seek to gain. If we don't feel worthy, there's a good chance nothing will happen. Haven't you bought a second book on positive thinking? Or did you get there in one go? Luck also may play a part, and luck is often enhanced by gratitude, good deeds, kind thoughts and a helping hand. You may also be born with it, some are and you could argue for decades about reincarnation and karma and whether this inherent good luck arises from past deeds in previous lives. It doesn't matter – you either have it or you don't, but you can develop it. That is the essence of positivity. But consider this.

Positive thinking at best exerts an influence on the world around us that will be to our benefit, a benefit willed and wished for and perhaps also worked hard for. After all, action is king. It's pointless wishing for manna and doing nothing to bring it closer to within your grasp. Are you with me there? If it's an actual thing or situation you wish for, you may have to do something about it after all the imaging.

Wishing for grace may be different and that will be because spirit will want to help you and will accompany you all the way along the path. Remember the footsteps in the sand, I walk alongside you. You may not even need to do anything at all to attain grace, it could suddenly come your way because you have so devotedly sought it and the whole of creation is behind your intent when it comes to grace. When it comes to physical things, spirit is more or less neutral, you can have it if you join up the dots and act positively. Grace is something else, spiritual awareness is something different, spirit in this case pulls out all the stops and eagerly wishes to bring you to where you want to go. You may also have to do something, but the odds are stacked in your favour. Pray, meditate, seek. You cannot go far wrong. And if manna is your thing, you could pursue that as well.

Here we fall into a common problem for spiritual seekers. Whether it is all right to have things when you're on a spiritual path. So many explain away poverty and say that wealth is unnecessary and detrimental to their soul's journey. In an ideal world they have a point, but we all have bills to pay as long as we're in physical form, which we are. I can't imagine there's many ascended masters reading this right now, and, yes, I do think they exist. I would say there's no problem at all to being rich or opulent and also a seeker as the spiritual realm is only interested in how you use it. Hoarding it is not ideal, as money or status is also meant to be to the benefit of others. Hoard your coins, put them in a hole in the ground, and they cannot do very much there for you or for anyone else. This has been said before. We live in an interconnected world and what we give to others we in some way or another give to ourselves. Which is not to advise making your own life subservient to the desires of others, no. We've touched on this earlier. In some ways, on all our paths, it pays to put our own needs and our spiritual requirements first.

Schopenhauer asserts that magical transformation, that is attaining what we wish for, is dependent on human will and not ritual. We may use ritual, sure – affirmations, posters, chanting and such, but it is for him a matter of will. Intent, determination, belief, I'm extrapolating here. And this ties in nicely with meditation followed up by action. It maybe doesn't tie in with grace, which is granted, given, bestowed, rather than worked hard for at an industrial level. We can still do things, yes, but ultimately we long for grace and it is gifted by a higher power which wishes us well and wants us to succeed.

16. Jumping and Programming

Why should I say this, if not through personal experience?

I have mentioned being in a river and suddenly being on a beam, without having done anything physical to get there. This was one of the defining moments of my thinking. Psychiatry is a true danger for those of us in the West who are on a spiritual path as in psychiatry spirituality in the west is all right as long as it's just words. When it gets to actions it's a different thing. What is acceptable, laudable even, in the East is frowned upon in the West. And that may be because we've given up any real belief in spirit. We say the words, we attend church, we may believe we have a spiritual life (we do), but we're not prepared to do much about it and, if we're in the medical profession, we're certainly not prepared to let anyone else do anything about it in the West. Psychiatry would say my experiences lie in my imagination. That, under stress, duress, I imagined the whole thing. That I'd buried the entirety of the event away from memory as it was all too traumatic and had spiritualised the ordinary. This is not at all true. Jumping into a river, when I first did it, was one of the calmest, most benign events in my life. I wanted to stay in the river, looking at the sky and when I did reach dry land I felt light and non-corporeal. I glided like a fairy, the weight of the physical simply didn't seem to be there.

That was an unforgettable and sometimes grieved over event as it suggested that I'd reached a real level of spirituality that I've certainly lost since and that is cause for regret. This was one spiritual event that I cannot deny and will not forget. It underlines everything that I say here because it was real. It differed from awareness, knowing, hearing or anything else as it was rooted in what we see as physical space and physicality, although of course it didn't follow any of the rules we know of. It went splendidly and beautifully against them.

So I have reason to believe in the power of spirit to affect the physical world we appear to live in and that is worth remembering. In every event we find ourselves in, there is a degree to which it is not real, it may be altered, it can be subject to grace.

We see what we are programmed to see, we expect what we are programmed to expect. Parental, societal, whatever root cause, we run programmes and may react strongly if our accepted programmes are questioned. We have, after all, formed our lives around them and may have made mistakes or had losses by depending on our world view and so we adher to our inputed belief systems all the more. We should try not to, as some programmes we run may not be doing us much good. It's the old chestnut of when prophesy fails. When our expectations fail we cling all the more to our past beliefs as we've invested so much in them. A bit like a marriage, we cling on and often our determination does work. That goes back to determination perhaps.

Apart from Schopenhauer, other thinkers who have shaped our worldview include Carl Sagan, an astronomer. He is quoted as saying:

"If we long for our planet to be important, there is something we can do about it. We make our world significant by the courage of our questions and by the depth of our answers."

Perhaps we could change that to:

*"If we long for our **lives** to be important, there is something we can do about it. We make our world significant by the courage of our questions and by the depth of our answers."*

We often don't do this, as the temptation and easy option is to cling to our past beliefs, even when failing. If we keep at it, surely, surely they must come true and sometimes, indeed, they do, which may be the law of averages. Like the geek who keeps asking people out – if you ask frequently enough, someone at sometime may say yes. So my advice would be to keep questioning and relax as somewhere the answers appear. Carl Sagan also said *""the universe seems neither benign nor hostile, merely indifferent to the concerns of such puny creatures as we are*" and you'll already guess I disagree as we, you and I, are not puny creatures. The universe is not indifferent, although it can be uninvolved. We are creatures of such power and such creativity that we do not want to look at that (as it imposes a certain responsibility). Instead we immerse ourselves in rules given by some greater person than we, some authority figure whom we follow, perhaps to our detriment. Such is the power of religions, and people do do horrendous things in thrall to their teachings. Is this spiritual? No need to reply.

17. Sight–Things Seen

I'm talking from personal experience, as otherwise you might not pay much attention to anything I'm saying – who am I and so on – and I'd like you to consider it and take some added awareness away with you. I've touched on physical experience which went against perceived laws of gravity but now I'd like to look at sight and what we see.

If we're lucky enough to see, we all more or less see the same things. That's a bit of a bummer as I'm arguing that nothing of what we see is real. So how come we're agreed on what's out there? To start with, we don't all agree. Some are born autistic and high-functioning people with autism can have cognitive and/or linguistic abilities that are in the average to above average range for their age. They may have difficulty interpreting social clues which is a common issue with autism. They don't see the world as most people do. In some cases, their perceptions are "better" – clearer, more specific, intense. I'm thinking of a young man who took a helicopter flight over London and from some minutes flight was able to draw and reconstruct the entire cityscape of London in architectural detail. That is something most of us can't do – maybe sometime, but not at present. Autistic people see things differently. Added abilities come with added difficulties – we would perceive that to be so. Mozart was said to be a bit odd.

Some of us experience colour blindness, where as many as one in twelve men are unable to tell the difference between red and green. They do not see colour as the rest of us would. Colour may be subjective in any case. Most of us agree on what is green, but what is our subjective experience of green? It may differ from one person to the next, there's no way of telling. Some of us may be seeing green in fluorescent flashing colour, or then again not, but you get my point. We are all similar in our perceptions but we're not always the same.

So, how subjective and personal is sight? Is it real? Can we at all rely on it? I'd like you to go beyond the science of eyesight for a moment. We all see things and perhaps see them differently but aren't aware of it, as I mentioned above. It doesn't affect our life that much, if at all, and we know how the eye operates, and if we don't we can look it up from reliable sources.

Now, I'm going to pose a question here – if we see something that isn't there, is it merely hallucination? Here again I'm writing from personal experience of seeing things that aren't – necessarily – there, or at least aren't there in this time frame and in this place. We look into the far distance and we see houses or trees, depending on where we're looking from. Industrial or verdant, we all generally accept that they're there and unchangeable and that what we see is real. In certain cases, yes, they are tangible. Sometimes not. When I was in full channelling mode, and that lasted for a long time, I saw things differently. I saw stars which certainly weren't there in any prosaic sense as they didn't merely twinkle, they sparkled and moved up and down outside my window. They were stunning and quite large - not just a mote of sparkle in the eye. And to my sight they were certainly there. So you will say this falls into the category of hallucination and I won't argue with you. I think it does. That they were uplifting and glorious and supportive is hardly here or there. I saw what I needed to see at that time, I saw them subjectively and needed and appreciated and talked much about them. I thought they were wonderful, a king, a queen, a knave, how we extrapolate, how we personify and give things human characteristics. I've a strong imagination and an intuitive nature. I am happy with my identification of king, queen, knave, but I will readily admit that in this instance I, too, accept these were products of my own imagination - but strongly visual products. I saw what may not have been there (I have to fudge this a bit, as I'm also aware in my understanding of reality that they may have been there).

Bear with me here as I'd like to tell you about another occasion that is not so easily explained.

I was in rural Wales, many years ago now, I was still quite young. I'd followed my instinct to go down and I was in a town that bordered England with a stream running nearby. A river perhaps, not large. On an unexplored pathway, I came to a small wall and was told not to go in. At that time I followed instruction more closely than I have done since. I was fully compliant, so I didn't. Behind the wall was a sloping grassy hill and on top of the hill there was a small golden castle. It was round, built of golden brick, one storey high and not very large. It looked beautiful and I gazed at it for some time. I was thinking King Arthur, knights, mediaeval England, the way you do in that part of the world because something about the atmosphere evokes the mystical, and it is a way of life (and a good source of income too) in that area. So I was happy with my meander and walked on to stand by the river and eventually make my way home, the way all good travellers eventually must. I remembered it vividly but thought little of it, apart from how pretty it all had been.

It was sometime later, on another visit, I went down again. Can you imagine what I saw? On the same route, in the same place, the golden castle on the hill was no longer there. Instead, in its place, stood an enormous

Norman castle, grey, imposing and several stories high. It had battlements and, yes, it stood on a grassy hill, but there the similarities ended. This is odd, I felt and I am in life used to the odd. I consider it almost normal, but worthy of mention just the same. What do you think? Are you willing to class this as hallucination? In one sense yes, of course. In another it meant that my eyes, as captors of what is real, just weren't working at all. My "imagination", if you will, had taken over. I saw what, for lack of a better term, someone else wanted me to see. And more importantly that the small golden castle that had been there was now the monumental grey one that stood there. It was simply unmissable – so you'd think. Doesn't it say something about our ability to see reality. Why did I not see what was so glaringly in front of me. How does an C11th castle vanish into thin air? That's the interesting question.

It means that our eyes are subject to our brain – they don't operate in any scientific way at all. Instead of functioning in linear fashion – object in, object seen – they simply don't operate at times. This has to be compelling as it means that something in the brain dictates what we see – or perhaps something outside of ourselves, and may explain why some other adventurers in life see things that others will say simply don't exist. It is all subjective, all unreal. You may not agree with this but I would like you to at least think about it, because sages through the ages have said simply this, that all is unreal. Reality around us does not exist. Second Corinthians, 4:18 "*While we look not at the things that are seen, but at the things which are not seen; for the things that are seen* **are** *temporal; but the things which are not seen* **are** *eternal*". There's a lot of good things in the bible and similarly a lot of rubbish has been extrapolated from it. Here in my off-the-cuff praise I'm a little like a mouse saying a lion is just a little larger, but it's a book, written by many people and open to interpretation and sometimes that interpretation has been a little skew-whiff. Here it is worth thinking about.

I won't rest my case, I may come back to quotations later, many people in many ages have sought for an answer to our existence and our wish, so fervent, to live in connection with a spiritual reality, which is, as I have said and others before me, all around us and willing to be found.

18. Backup Authors–Great for Dinner Parties

Here I'd like to seek out backup just a little as you may find it interesting to see what others, in other terms or at other times, have said about our inner world. So I'm including a few more quotes, that say more or less the same thing – a bit specious to say that, as I've chosen the quotes in a search for quotes that would fit in, so of course they fundamentally agree. Nonetheless.

Herman Hesse was a German novelist who was interested in exploring the search for authenticity. He was talking about our inner world when he said: "*There is no reality except the one contained within us. That is why so many people live such an unreal life. They take the images outside them for reality and never allow the world within to assert itself.*" We mistake what we see outside for reality.

We need to go inwards before we can have any real standing outside ourselves, otherwise all is unsure and built on sand. Matthew 7 (Catholic and Protestant bible) says that a wise man builds his house upon a rock and that rock is surely going within and gaining self-knowledge in order to position ourselves more confidently in the world and for others. It's not just self-knowledge. If we go within, we have time and space to hear from spirit and connect with the spiritual world which lies outside and within and which we so, so much want to connect with, even though we may not see it or word it that way. When we feel emptiness, when we are alone, when we are in thrall to addiction of any kind, we are desperate to connect with the real world that lies all around us and that we can at least in part access, the world of spirit. Matthew says "*and the rain descended and the floods came and the winds blew and beat upon that house and it fell not, for it was founded upon a rock*".

Lao Tzu is said to be a Chinese philosopher born around the early centuries of the Christian era, though there is some doubt as to whether he was one person or his writings were the accumulation of many Taoist writers, so we can with impunity say that we don't know a great deal about him as it's unclear that he existed, which is great for appearing erudite at supper parties, ah yes, Lao Tzu – or not. No matter, his words bear a great deal of weight to my mind and possibly now to yours. Here we go, for a non-existent writer he made wonderful sense: "*the key to growth is the introduction of higher dimensions of consciousness into our awareness*".

And we do that by taking time, going within, contemplating, meditating, praying, there are many ways and most of them involve space, peace, silence. I know music can help, gong music, spiritual music, I personally find it takes away from the experience of going within a little, I prefer silence, but your way of accessing spirit may be different. Spirit has come through to me big time in the cinema, in amongst the popcorn and loud ads, I move into a different world entirely, one where movement is impossible or it would break the spell, one where spirit speaks directly to me, one where it would be absolutely impossible to earn a living or fill in a tax return, which is awkward for our day-to-day lives, but spirit stays with us for these too. If I move, the spell breaks. I need to stay within, stay silent and all the rest becomes unreal. The true reality, our only reality, lies within.

You can doubt what I'm saying, but I'm not alone in saying it. But try silence, try meditation, even if you have no seeming success, no words coming through, you will feel calmer, more resolute, more able to face the various challenges in your life, if there are any. For sometimes we reach a stage where challenges don't seem to apply so much. They become just another part of life and one we can more easily face. If you doubt this, I couldn't put doubt better than J.M. Barrie who wrote Peter Pan, the story about the little boy who could fly. He said that "*the moment you doubt whether you can fly, you cease forever to be able to do it*". I think that's a little harsh and that at every moment we can make a decision that can reverse things. You may never get back to the point of flying, that moment may have passed forever, but we can in other ways fly and gain something of the same wonder and optimism again, as if we were a child preparing for take-off.

"Real work is completed in silence and strikes a chord in the minds of only a very few".

C.G. Jung.

19. Going Within and Donegal

When I speak about landscape, I feel it very keenly. Place to me is important. Perhaps that should not be so, but where I am has an influence on how I feel. All experience is subjective, and resonates with our past, so landscapes from my childhood evoke a lot. I see again my parents and grandparents on distant Donegal shores. In this case, I don't actually see them but I know that they are there and I gain, once again, the feeling of youth and growing up in a society I loved. It was a divided society and I was drawn to the opposite pole of things. I lived among them and was lucky to do so, while on the prosaic side of things I was schooled amongst the other pole, which was where I was said to "belong", although I never really did. This dichotomy perhaps saved me from a polarised view of life rooted in ancestral problems and broadened my mind – which then became broader through life experience. I'm not without narrow belief systems, but I have fewer than many and that is because I took the risk and explored life, both within and without. Exterior and interior experience has shaped who I am and for the most part I am very happy with me.

I think quite a few people are not so and that is one reason I am writing this book – to provide levitation of mind if not of body. We are who we are. We are all quite similar but superficially may appear very distinct. We are all souls. I try now when I meet people to view them as souls. This makes it easier to empathise with people who may be different in some way. Mainly I succeed. With this view in life it becomes easier to relate to all, in the way Christ did. Mary Magdalene was not out of bounds – although some say the original Christian teachings emanated from her and she was the essential leader of Christianity in a hidden way, we don't know for sure but we can be bloody sure that if she was it got buried over in some way. Christ is said to have sat down with all. He spoke to the Samaritan woman at a well. Jews didn't generally do this. He was open to all and conversed with all and had time for all (except for money changers) and in general was open minded. It's not a bad approach. I know in the developmental world that some say we should mix with those of like mind, those we can learn from, those we most want to develop into – but that is when it comes to making wealth. We can monitor and copy and succeed. And there is the idea too that our earnings are equal to the earnings of those we most socialise with, to around 10% or so. What they and we earn reflects what we think we should earn and our decisions and actions are influenced by those around us. But this is the approach of children, is it not, who reflect and absorb the ideas of their elders. We tend to do this, and to blend in with those around us, to an astonishing and often detrimental degree. Women in many societies have been expected to serve and in many societies, even in the west, they still do. They may have the trappings of independence, but they are subservient to the wishes, desires and at times rage of those around them. They become victimised because they have become separated from who they actually are as individuals, as have the men who victimise them. They have lost touch, or never developed touch, with their own ideas, their own wishes, their own passionately held view of how they would like their life to develop, we all do that and some break loose, a little or a lot, and society views them in terms of this, as acceptable or out of bounds. Because we *are* out of bounds, those of us who have learned to think differently. When folk become separate from their own desires, they turn inward, while acting almost exclusively outwards. They resort to gossip, one-up-manship, the exteriors of life, because deep inside they *know* they have not explored how they are, they are out of touch with their needs. It's highly approved of by society but it's not a good approach. It may produce comfortable and acceptable lives but it ends with frustration. A lot goes back to talents, the different gifts and inclinations we are all blessed with which, if we turn our back on, lead to lives less lived than they might have been. I mentioned earlier that we don't have to *succeed* at being ourselves, but I think even a step in this direction goes far as it comes with the full backing of spirit and full recognition by our inner voice which knows who we are and could become. And it leads to satisfaction, even small steps towards who you actually are can bring great results. If you haven't already done so, try listening to your inner voice and following what it says. It is never too late.

Going within provides an impetus to follow our own path, which we all have. We have different imprints one from another and different pathways and when we reach the end of our life, we shall feel satisfied to the degree that we have taken these routes and followed these desires and made something original and wonderful - or a dog's dinner, it little matters as at least we shall have tried. Success is nice though and spirit does put pointers on our path. Roads less travelled are interesting, dangerous, supported and worth setting out on.

Still, I go back to the past and it nourishes me in a way that little else does. The hills, the light, the bright waters and the accents, the sandy beaches, the little shells, the basalt columns, the coves, the gorse and the fuchsia, the yellow lillies and the forts on hills, Grainin of

Aileach, bird sanctuaries with wild swans at the entrance to Inishowen, white houses, turf stacks, dark bog water and wild cotton growing, small strawberries in among the dunes, all of this to me connects me to God. Which was what I wanted all along. I could just have stayed put.

I am dedicating this book to my brother who has been with me on this pathway for most of my life, although he lives his path differently, the aims and destinations are, I think, the same. To him too, gardens, flowers, hills and expansive views nourish his soul and lift his spirit.

May they do the same for all of you, but we are different as well as similar, and your source of soul may come in music, in art, in love, we all take different paths - and we all end up in more or less the same place. The awareness of which brings us through.

20. Messages for Others.

I feel I should write this book because I hear from spirit all the time. Mainly these are words that uplift me and sometimes they are, as I mentioned earlier, words spoken in a detached manner that say it as it is – somewhat condemnatory, I realise that. I accept this and would much sooner hear these words than not. A world without a spiritual connection is at this time unthinkable. I could do it, but so much would be missing. So they support, suggest, nudge at times strongly and at those times, which are not so frequent as I am allowed an enormous degree of self-determination, I've found it better to go along with spirit because where it is insistent it doesn't give up. If it's insistent about something today it will be doubly insistent tomorrow, so it's better to go along with it and know that it is for someone's best advantage.

I say someone's because on very – very – rare occasions I get messages through for someone else. Let me tell you about these, they are so infrequent that they are worth mentioning. I can think of two cases where I was resistant but spirit insisted. They are not huge in themselves but I went along with it. I am not a medium, so I felt foolish and realised in context I might appear odd for following through, but I kept with it.

The first was in a coffee shop from my childhood overlooking an arcade. I was about to leave, having finished a small lunch and coffee and saw coming in an older woman, rather stern, conservatively dressed. The shop was filled with high-end fashion that would suit such a one as she appeared to be, quite expensive, altogether smart and not too outstandish. I was given some words to give to her. Now, she in no way looked upset or disturbed, she was quite poised and she went to sit on the balcony level. I progressed through the dress shop towards the exit on my way towards avoidance. Go back, quite strong in tone, so I turned round and did just that. Much against my will I have to add, as she was having coffee with two younger people and I felt, oh so keenly, that I would be viewed as an intruder. I stood beside her, excused myself for speaking with her, and said simply that spirit had a message for her. There is support there for you in spirit, I said, as those were the words I had heard. And it is a lovely message, is it not, to be told that when you are on your morning coffee would be quite nice to hear, I think. Where we were has quite a conventional approach to life, it's deeply ingrained, so she wanted to know what spirit was. Was it God? I'm always hesitant to say God, for I don't see life in that way, so I simply said it was from spirit. What else did it say?

Again, I can't add or detract from what has been given to me, I said that there was no further message that it meant simply she was supported by spirit. If I'd been a medium on the take, I might have added some further embellishment, invited her to a cult meeting, a lecture, a book tour, something gainful. I had none of this in mind. I simply told her what had been told to me, that there was support there for her in spirit. The other people there looked on. Something different.

She asked me about myself, did I know so and so as I had said I was from the area, and told me too then that her husband of many years had died from Covid just some months earlier. That was nice to hear as it gave a reason for the message, I thought, and I gave her my sympathy and left. Still feeling a little foolish.

Now, you might think that I simply picked up on some emanation of grief, some subtle signal, but I swear that outwardly there were none. Yes, I'm empathetic, yes, I pick up signals and I do so intuitively as well as psychologically, in other words I pick up psychically and not just from psychological tells, such as hunched shoulders, an air of grief, there was none of that. I simply did what spirit told me to and felt better for it. I hope so did she. I still felt a bit of a fraud as if I were play acting as an older medium, the Madame Arcati of the coffeeshop, but in a sense that's always what I wanted to be. Just for the main part it doesn't happen for me like that.

That was the first occasion and there is one other I want to tell you about, when spirit intervened in a big way. The first occasion was not breathtaking in any way, this one was. Let me tell you about it.

There I was, as we do, thinking over something in my life and deciding to confront someone because I felt she'd been a bit off with me. Wouldn't do and so on. I was in bed in the morning – yes, it's the number one time for sleep paralysis and feeling someone is in the room. I'll give you that, if you're of sceptical mind, it is that. What I experienced on waking surprised me so much that it will probably resonate with me for the rest of my days. A voice spoke and said simply "With love". The thing about it was that this voice wasn't in my head, it was in the room. She spoke as clearly as if you had been standing by my side and said something in my ear. Loud and clear. "With love". It turned out to be a very accurate message as the person I'd been mulling over was going through a difficult time that I didn't know about. Saying something would have added to her trouble and fallen on totally disinterested ears. Who was I to bother about at that time in her life? No-one. So you see, I avoided falling flat on my face and causing someone I liked added torment. Just because I felt peeved, pissed off. Let's think about what we do when we're in that state as some things cannot be undone. They can be forgiven sure, frequently are, but forgotten? Never.

So I was saved from my own self-importance. An important message in itself. Turns out it wasn't just intended for me. Over the next few days I was pushed by spirit in an insistent manner. I was to contact a cleric I knew vaguely and tell him about it. I really didn't want to as I suspected he'd be abrasive. I had better things to be doing like visiting Las Vegas or having my hair done, anything really to avoid following through. The psychic realm doesn't fit well with some doctrines, although I don't know why that should be as the bible is full of it. Think of Daniel, think of Moses, think of the Witch of Endor, though maybe not as she was a prophecy of doom. I thought I'd be dismissed and that is what happened. Well, you got the result you expected he said, several times. Yes, I said, I did. He told me my message was not-acceptable, abhorrent, I've forgotten now the word he used, it was quite learned and I think he expected me not to know what it meant. Inimical, that was it, I've remembered it since. It's not a word that trips lightly off the tongue but I knew what it meant. It wasn't the pastoral approach. He was a clever man and thought that I was not. I repeated what I had said and continued to say she spoke just two words when she came through. She said with love and that got through. I think it connected with prayer. The man on the phone changed to softness, he went from difficult to humane. He laughed softly and we left it there. I know it was important and I know it was meant for him. Don't ask me how that knowingness manifests, I really couldn't say, you know what you are meant to do. Spirit sometimes doesn't give up. It hadn't given up on him and was urgently wanting to connect in a direct way.

And we do often, if we listen, if we truly listen we often hear our own wisdom or that of others. It can save us from many a tricky situation that we otherwise fall into as a result of habit or absence of thought. I've been as liable to this as anyone.

21. Knowing in Advance about Relationships

That leads me on to talk about relationship, or a particular facet of relationship we are prone to fall into if we really don't listen to our inner voice. I believe we know in advance what we're going for when we get into a relationship. In some instances difficulty might benefit us and we might actively choose it without being aware, but perhaps we don't need to go there if we acknowledge what we already know. We might avoid all disturbance if we listen to ourselves and our inner knowing. We do know, we do have an idea, and we at times just don't pay it any heed. Perhaps we haven't been in a relationship for a while and we feel if we don't act now, it could be years before one comes along – and it could be, take it from me. So in this instance perhaps action and commitment is best, at least you're doing something, learning something, but it's something you already know, so why go through the whole routine of learning it again?

This is true of one kind of relationship in particular, and while not rare it's mercifully not true of all.

Occasionally you might feel like drawing someone in even though you might not like them. True loving relationships are often easy from the get go. In cases such as this you might hesitate but feel drawn to pursuing them, gaining their alliance, entering into relationship with them. Watch this. If there is no real feeling of liking, rather a need to subdue into submission, then this is what this relationship is about. Something about the other person reminds you of someone in your past. It might not be obvious but it can be compelling. If you've been much criticised in your past you might draw in someone who is oh so supportive to begin with but who can turn out to be critical. In this relationship you will struggle as you try to overcome the other person, to make him or her love you, to gain their commitment and here's the not so surprising thing, once you have their love or affection your task is completed. You have won the earlier battle and you will leave. You may do this gradually. You will withdraw, you will go off sex, the person who was compelling leaves you cold. You may even grow to actively dislike them. That's because that person was not really for you in the first place but you felt a familiarity. Of course you did. You were reliving an earlier trauma Maybe you were either ready for a relationship, or needed to be successful in gaining their attention. By winning them over you succeed in the earlier relationship too. You become a winner where you felt previously a victim. If you're prone to this sort of thing, don't push relationships. A good one might well be easy, sure you'll learn from each other but mutual liking and support is quite a good way to go in life. Sod the difficult, don't take it as a challenge, just avoid it. This sort of relationship could even turn to hate and could be quite damaging to both parties, so keep an eye out, as you know what you need, but your small child may still be fighting battles it would be wiser to leave unturned. Enter relationships from a point of love.

That's the psychological bit out of the way.

On an intuitive level, I've said already that we know in advance what we're going for in a relationship, and in these difficult cases this too is true. You know what's coming up, it's just not obvious to you.

What is even more interesting is that, alongside knowing *what is* going to happen, we may know *when* we are going to get into a relationship. In two of my three major relationships this was the case for me. I knew keenly that that person was coming in, before I had met them or had any idea what they were like. Here's how – well, it's not an instruction manual so I can't tell you how to do it, but here's what happened to me and it indicates very clearly that spirit is at work and we can and should listen to it.

I was in my thirties when I was called to interview for a job. I *knew* that the person interviewing me would be important in my life and that I would most likely be in relationship with him. I knew absolutely nothing about who it was or what it would entail, I didn't even know his name. Call me psychic – well, yes. I liked him when I got to interview, I felt a connection. This wasn't because of any prior "knowing" or fulfilment of prophecy, I simply liked him. And so the relationship developed on line with expectation and was one of the more important of my life. The energy between us was easy, it was liking, mutual admiration, attraction, all the things you want. The situational aspects were less easy and perhaps I learned from them, certainly they were difficult, but the energy between us never was. We were pretty much ideal for each other. And I had known that beforehand.

I do believe that we may have contracted to enter into partnership with certain people in advance. Way in advance and for a period of time. If you view life this way, you can see why a loved relationship might split up. You hadn't contracted for any longer, parting is part of your learning process, the love remains but the relationship might go and that's not easy. Looking back though you can see that that person and that time were seminal to your life and to your understanding and to your future wellbeing in that you know you were loved and you accept that life flows. We cannot force it to take the shapes we would like. We can do everything in our power to make it a good relationship, but if it falls apart, maybe it was intended to. That may be wishful thinking, but as an approach it makes life somewhat easier as you get closer to its end. You were loved, someone cared enough, for whatever length of time you lived, loved and felt closer to spirit. I come back to that always, a nurturance of approach, a willingness to be alone, and I quote again Schopenhauer who appears to have been intelligent: "*To live alone is the fate of great souls*". If I extrapolate to sound less puffed up here, perhaps you could say that only someone in touch with their inner self is accepting of being alone.

What about relationship two, if you remember that in two cases I knew in advance that I would meet someone? It's a bit of a drag hauling this out but I do it to prove a point. You cannot extrapolate from a sample of one. So for the statisticians among you who would resolutely agree with that statement here's the second example. The rest of you are already on board.

Well, relationship two was different in that I wasn't going for an interview, I was going to bed. It was early in the evening and I was tired. Then a voice came, and at that time I was used to following voices. It told me to get up, get dressed and go down to a certain pub in the locality, one I never drank in and in case of doubt I'm not a big drinker. There I would find my husband said the voice. So I did what any sensible psychic would do, I got dressed and went out. I was in my forties. At this stage in my life I might well stay in bed. At the bar I met a man who again was to become important in my life. So much so that we remained in touch for many decades after we split up, in a supportive and affectionate relationship that was distanced. We did not see each other. I ended that aspect too, after being told in no uncertain terms by spirit to do so. It was, at the time, quite a challenge and I couldn't imagine not being in touch, but it was a good decision and I felt clearer, more authentic. It can be daunting, but generally it's best to go along.

I'm telling you this because in two out of three of three major relationships I had known in advance that I was about to meet someone. The information came in before the person.

22. Hierarchies in Spirit

That brings me on to hierarchies. What is spirit, who were these people who were giving me advice and instruction? How were they structured, how many could fit on the head of a pin? You know how it goes and here is what I think and it may, naturally, be entirely wrong, but this is the gist of it as far as I've got. There is a spiritual hierarchy. I really didn't want that to be the case. It doesn't fit with my view of spirit as a general energy that wants us to get closer and is caring for us, but in somewhat a dispassionate way. Spirit doesn't do oh dear, let me heal your wounds. Although it does walk beside us. It offers us a way out, one that may involve some discomfort or some learning, it supports us in our search for itself, in our yearning to get back, but it is neutral. It walks alongside us in the sand and at times carries us, but it doesn't engage too much with our struggles. It simply is. Hierarchy, the very term sounds earthly, structured, old-fashioned. It sounds bureaucratic.

And yet my experience suggests that is the case, and I struggle with that a little. I mentioned the Lady who came through to me early one morning and told me to act with love. She was dispassionate, yet a certain quality of personality came through with those two words. She was much higher in understanding than I was, but she had a vested interest, I would say, in my taking the higher path. Well, obviously, or she wouldn't have bothered to come through. She had a personality. And it seemed to me that she had a vested interest on her own behalf as well. How can you tell that from just a seconds surprise ? We pick up many things as children and as adults, that we mightn't realise. Our antennae are much more honed than we credit them to be, we just don't pay them much heed at times, which can work out to our detriment. Follow your instincts is often wise advice, so that is what I picked up, a Lady who was high in spirit and who may have had her own reasons for coming through. Not just a helpful, watchful presence, but someone who, yes, had her own path to tread.

I don't have much more to go on but that alone raised a dilemma, because I really don't do hierarchies. It makes sense in the meaning of spirit guides, gurus, holy men and women, angelic realms, hierarchies of heavenly choirs, all the religious stuff I'd rather dispensed with on my journey towards knowledge, but all stuff that the church bangs on about. I still don't go along with much of it, but I'm open to an hierarchical spiritual world now in a way I wasn't previously and it really isn't where I wanted to be.

I don't know about your life and your beliefs. Are they traditional or unconstrained? Are you New Age or conventional? Do you think about your inner life at all or is it all a bit of an inconvenience? It can be if it interferes with the direction you think your life should go. Sometimes it will take you on an altogether different path, but somewhere in your inner makeup that pathway is written already, and you sense that it is truth, you just hadn't got the courage to go there yet. Yet is quite a persuasive word. There's lots of life that's sacrificed to that little word. I haven't got around to it yet. And we all need rest, and we all need to rest on our laurels, be they shining or somewhat wilted, they're still ours, and we all need courage, courage to go within and double courage to follow what they say. Because they are saying, just mentioning that.

23. Being Geo-Centric

Carl Sagan said this: "*Those afraid of the universe as it really is, those who pretend to non-existent knowledge and envision a Cosmos centred on human beings will prefer the fleeting comforts of superstition. They avoid rather than confront the world. But those with the courage to explore the weave and structure of the Cosmos, even where it differs profoundly from their wishes and prejudices, will penetrate its deepest mysteries.*"

If you think I'm quoting this to back up my earlier argument about courage sometimes lacking, I'm not. It's interesting in that it goes against much of what I'm saying, because the entire New Age movement and much of what I'm arguing here is centred on human beings. We do not view the cosmos as a whole extensive set of planets, we see spiritual energy as centred on ourselves as human beings and on our afterlife. We're very ego centric. We have a vast and diverse set of religions and ways of thinking that have expansive spiritual realms focused on us, our welfare, our development. Even if, as in my case, we see spirit as somewhat distinct, we still feel it reaches out a hand, offers a pathway, illuminates a little on our path – it focuses on us. This, according to Carl Sagan, is superstition and I suppose he may be right.

The world of science looks at what is demonstrably there – although it sometimes really, really isn't. So we are at odds and we cannot know for sure which approach is right. It harms us not at all to believe in a spiritual reality if we can balance it with equitable behaviour and love towards others. So we might as well believe, I guess, because science can be a cold bedfellow, whereas an archangel overlooking your interests might be of some solace in the dark of night. Enlightenment may have turned some of the switches off. And if spirituality exists, as it certainly does in the inner wishes of us all, then we might as well believe in it, because if it doesn't exist our disbelief won't get us far anyway. Lights out and back to the dark ages, which is where we really don't want to be as we've grown used, all of us, to being our own inner guides.

There is little new in this. Pascal – C17th French Catholic mathematician – was coming out of the dark ages when he said that it was more rational to choose belief in God (in modern terms I prefer spirituality), even if there's no scientific evidence. He considered it a more pragmatic approach to choose to believe as, as I've said above, you've nothing to lose and are truly in a win-win situation, rather than a lose-lose one if you don't believe and even turn out to be right. Camus, French writer years later, said much the same thing. *"I would rather live my life as if there is a God and die to find out there isn't, than live as if there isn't and to die to find out that there is*". Both are advocating a life guided by moral principle. This goes back to the idea that it is better to live with a spiritual framework than without one. Both men predate us by quite a bit and lived in a highly religious environment. In our times, quite a number of writers are arguing that we are close to a breakthrough spiritually and that may be the case. It appears that the old structures are or have been corrupt and that leaves the way for more self-determination, less hierarchy, more inner searching and, if you go inwards, you find, of course, spirit and your own way of leading a life that is more meaningful for you - and not just appropriate to the community within which you live. The two are not incompatible, for highly spiritual people may find it not too difficult to blend in, but they may also hide their views under compliance which is fairly detrimental I feel to themselves and those around them, who live without a certain light that may raise questions. A certain enlightenment of spirit that, as I said, may be coming in, or may not. We have no way of knowing for sure, sometimes things can go one way or the other. What is sure is that the more of us who go within in a search for spirit and the answers it offers, the more likelihood of a shift in human consciousness for the better - or I may just be viewing things from a morally smug Western viewpoint, we who are fairly safe and secure in our outer life have the luxury of delving within, but this is a luxury that is open to all, is it not, and one that can often be found in the depths or turmoil and despair. Spirit shines through and may illuminate a meaning to existence that we would previously not have thought of - or relied on.

24. The New Age Movement and the Secret

I'm an expert on New Age writers. I may not be too hot on Schopenhauer or Pascal, but mention a New Age name and I'm there. Since the age of 13 I've read it all. I started early and never stopped. Has it worked, you ask? To a degree, it's certainly brought about a different approach to life as I am now more pro-active, more inclined to start on projects I might previously have thought not possible. I've looked with interest at books on positivity, creative thinking, channelling, spiritual development, self-improvement, how to get rich and gain friends and influence people, one of the original best sellers. All of these mainly come down to the same thing. Believe in yourself, believe in spirit and take action. Maybe not all of them require a belief in spirit, but it underlies a great many of these practices. Take action are the two words that stand out. You can sit and wait for the big drop into your lap, some do, and you may succeed, but it goes against the odds. How much better to take action. I remember a large – thousands – group session where we all stood and shouted out "take action". Initially I was appalled, later I joined in. It's very good advice, even if you're not quite sure where you're going at least if things don't work out you'll know what path not to follow in future. Thomas Edison, American inventor, said this: *"I have not failed, I've just found 10,000 ways that don't work"*. Trying is not a waste of time, what is a waste of time or at least of success is sitting thinking you don't need to do anything. There are folk who are born to be wealthy. So this advice does not initially apply to them, they could sit on a dung heap and discover it held within it a nugget of gold and quite a few people fall into that category. It's not at all rare. He's always lucky is a phrase you might hear of someone who has succeeded without much apparent effort. You could argue that they paddle beneath the water, but there are people who are successful without much paddling at all. In these cases be thankful on their behalf but just think how much more they could achieve with even minimum paddling in an intuitively based direction. I'm not hot on religion, as you'll discover, but the bible talks about not sitting on your laurels, not hiding your gold in the ground, not disregarding your talents. Success is not the main aim in life I should say here, but it is a truth that successful people sometimes achieve more. Not just the fruit of their success, but an ability to make contact with others through connections they can make. Connection to spirit probably is the main aim in life, but we live in a prosaic world that appears real and requires action of some sort, so even if you're successful without much effort you'll probably find you want to *do* something. Even gurus who turn inwardly and who fast are doing quite a lot, inwardly if not outwardly.

Let me quote Pablo Picasso who said that everything you can imagine is real. This is a huge part of our reality though often we don't realise it and it lies at the root to the new thinking business of positivity. Think and grow rich, the secret to turning your life around, all of that and more. The root cause to happiness is thinking and believing that it is possible for you to be happy. Many of us don't expect that, we've been brought up to believe otherwise or formative experiences have coloured our expectations, and this can work either way but here we're talking about people who don't believe they can be happy and who are therefore creating a life in which they almost certainly won't be or if they happen upon happiness may lose it again. Well, that can happen to all of us at any stage, but here we're talking about likelihood. The likeliest outcome and I'm suggesting it pays off to envisage the most beneficial outcome you possibly can, and it do no harm, and then act upon it. Results may take years, growing a successful business, or may come about in minutes, finding a fiver in the road.

The Secret, a relatively recent book, explores this and acknowledges its debt to previous thinkers from an earlier age. It's not an entirely new idea. The reason behind it is something I'd like to look at in more depth. It's all right to say and believe that spirit is behind us and will support us in our positive endeavours, but it's a little vague and ties in, a little too closely I think, with our notion of God. I do believe in a spiritual reality and that on the whole it supports us if we allow it to, but my concept of reality is a little less solid. I believe from personal experience that nothing around us is real, I've had experience of this and that the life we lead is our creation, although not entirely. We think, we believe and we create. "*As you have believed so shall it be done onto you*", again a sensible teaching from the Christian bible. Books like the Secret suggest various ways we can shore up our beliefs and bring them to pass, but they don't generally say that nothing, but nothing around us is real. It is all entirely a simulacrum which we through thought and action have brought to pass.

Think of, possibly apocryphal stories, of men and women doing impossibly strong physical feats at a time of immense danger, of things working out exactly as planned, of Lottery winners who know in advance, absolutely know, that they have won and this, involving a much smaller prize, happened also to me. It is hard to manufacture the degree of certainty that was involved, as I absolutely knew that I had won the raffle. It hadn't happened before and hasn't happened since, but it worked out exactly as I *knew* it would. It's hard to replicate.

You might argue that we've incorporated quite a lot of suffering in our world view, and that is so, as we're not ascended masters and doubt and totally awful sins like greed, envy and hatred get in the way. Sin is a rather awkward word but when you look at what we *could* create and what we *have* created, it's not far off our reality. We sin against what we could be, what we could create, what we could envisage, either because we're lazy or because we just don't know any better, often the latter.

I don't believe in original sin and I doubt many modern clerics do either. There is though a degree to which we are bound to our birth and carry with us traits and potential life experiences that will occur, but the degree to which they occur and the way in which they do so is highly malleable. It will be different for all of us as none of us have the same challenges or benefits in life, but it will be there. To a degree therefore you could say that original sin, or better yet, original challenge does exist. I've said earlier that we meet challenges in different ways at different times depending on how well we have developed, how much attention we have paid to pointers on our path because they are there. Do we continue to create the same patterns again and again and fail each time or do we recognise a pattern as raising its head, oh here it comes again, and react somewhat differently leading to a more positive or successful outcome? Hopefully we do.

For me it's a certainty that people come into life with patterns well ingrained. You can preach about environment to your heart's content and it does have a considerable effect, but the ingrained patterns are with you from day one and, to a certain extent, your potential life's path is also laid out. If you understand the patterning you may and can alter the outcomes over time, but they always present as a danger, a potential trap into which you might automatically fall if you fail to exercise due diligence. Be alert, be very alert, your country needs lerts. Sorry, can't resist, the odd slip. So if you're patterned for jealousy and then, just then, happen to be born into a family where your younger brother/sister is feted and praised and you feel just a little ordinary, then the jealousy will be heightened, but believe me it is there from the start. Jealousy is not something we are all born with, some have it more than others and so, yes, the conditioning we receive activates it or not, but it is inherent in some and the risks are always there. So raising your own personal awareness can only do good, and it is this that most of the self-help movement is built upon. *"Knowing yourself is the beginning of all wisdom"* said Aristotle and to take it further, Laozi, founder of Taoism, said that knowing others is intelligence, knowing yourself is true wisdom. Mastering others is strength, mastering yourself is true power. And that is what much of the self-help industry is about, mastering yourself, either through exercises, meditation, decision taking, action, lists, visualisations, chanting, it's quite a lot of work and for some or many it does work, or it brings in results that are sometimes propitious.

The New Age movement doesn't, too often, look at why positivity might be useful, other than to say that spirit supports us in our every endeavour and that what we give out comes back to us, either in terms of evil doing, or of positive intent - backed by action. That's it in a nutshell. Decide, imagine, act and all this shall be yours.

My take on all of this is the following. It can work, it can work splendidly and sometimes if you have a wobble or try too hard, or don't follow up on ideas or hunches, it doesn't work and then you jack it all in and go back to bread and coffee. Smelling the coffee's fine, gratitude is a mighty thing, but there is potential out there for all of us if we just pursue it. Or it can work in the wrong direction, where you feel you should open up a business, say, and put into practice everything you have learned, and ignore feelings of oh I absolutely hate my time here but I'm doing so well, just look, and that may be because you *ab initio*, from the start, decided on the wrong route for you because it looked like the right route for so many others. Look before you commit because these routines for success do work.

This sounds like work, as I've said. Well, anything, including writing this book, can seem like work but if you like what you're doing and believe in your positive outcome, it won't so much. You probably won't get rich doing something you absolutely hate, though in material terms you may get comfortable. If you hate it you won't have the enthusiasm or intent to keep at it for the hours required, you won't live and breathe it, you won't get a sense of excitement from it. If nothing else, do something you quite like. Because what you like will have a link to what you're good at and a link too to what you're *meant* to be doing. And there is nothing, nothing, that brings more joy than excelling at what you're meant to be doing from a spiritual point of view.

You see, we do create our own reality, but to a degree most, if not all, self-help books don't dwell on irreality. My belief and my experience is that nothing, but nothing, in our world is real. And I'd like to look at that for a bit, for we create it all. Every last bit of it, including what is in our immediate vicinity and what is out there worldwide. Every soul can achieve a lot and so what if it appears to be limited to neighbourhood things, if you're on line with your intended life, your success will spread out and affect others. Butterfly effect and so on, and you're part of the whole.

25. We are Gods

Why is nothing real? Nothing is real because we ourselves are spiritual beings with a strong ability to create. We do this in an entirely (world view) acceptable way by acting on inbred or incoming influences and thus creating for ourselves lives of distress or comfort. It varies from time to time, for all of us, up and down. This is accepted by the main stream and so we have psychotherapy in action, delving deep into past influences in an attempt to change our reactions and thereby change our outcomes. So far, so good. It's relatively new, but the idea of having succour brought to our problems through the auspices of an outside source (your therapist) is not. Witchcraft has relied on this for centuries, so has the church. Pray, buy a relic, attend worship, sip this herb concoction, attend this voodoo ceremony, wear an amulet, all of these are based on an ability to heal ourselves which in these cases is based on an outside source, a backup authority to rely on and feel confident in. The outside comes in to support us in a way that society can accept - though may not entirely approve of at times and customs vary according to time -but they all depend on the external. In the New Age view you are inwardly responsible for outcomes which you yourself can adjust through the power of thought, although here too they depend on reliance on outside sources, diet, exercise, chanting, charity, prayer. Now, prayer I'm quite in favour of, but the others are optional and certainly not the main source of a happy outcome to any problems you may *perceive* yourself as having.

I suggest, as I wholeheartedly believe - that all of these possible sources of cure or happiness are back up structures only to enable us to access what is causing most, if not all, of our issues in life - our own inner power, our link to the divine. I'm not ruling out the divine or fate entirely, as I think I've touched on, they are powerful influences, but we ourselves are gods. We create. We do it mainly unconsciously at present, or attribute successful outcomes to the studies we have relied on and the rituals we have proceeded with. Because of all this, meditation, reflection, ways of improving physical well-being, all of this is a ritual and we continue with it in expectation of a happier outcome.

If it works, it's because we ourselves are the authors of our wellbeing, our future selves, and we know it but oftentimes turn away from our knowledge, dismissing hints from our unconscious, ignoring dreams, bearing up with feelings of frustration because we deserve nothing better, turning away from the path of our higher selves, our potential life lived in line with the spiritual reason we are in the world. We miss our calling and so feel frustration, which we alleviate with outside entertainment, addictions, travel whatever. There are a myriad ways of distraction out there and we all indulge to greater or lesser degrees. It can be daunting to pursue what you know or feel strongly to be your life's calling. Who doesn't need a little light relief from time to time?

26. Nothing is Real–Ecclesiastes

Now I've looked at most of the New Age sources out there. I've listened to The Secret, heard the ideas of most of the world's New Age teachers, both on the Secret's tapes and elsewhere, and the same names crop up time and again. As they have done over decades, only the names change from time to time as older teachers fade out and new ones take their place and each decade the stress alters, at one stage reincarnation, channelling, then as times change, the universe, our own personal power, think and become - though this latter one has been around for at least one hundred years as it was very prevalent in writings from the 1920s. There's not much out there that I've missed. And I've noticed latterly, because I've been looking for it, that there is - at least - one thing missing from all the teachings. Any information about the universe. There is a universal energy that supports us and in which we have to trust. This is what is said. We act as if we already have what we desire and then we take action knowing that the universe will support us. This is completely fine and I recommend that you read up on it and pursue if you haven't already done so.

However, I suspect that in reaching for the title of this book you may already have read up quite a lot and are wondering, perhaps, why it's not working or how it works or whether there's something missing, a missing link, which is the title of this book.

So what is this missing link? The law of attraction says "*we can create it if we want it*". How do we do this? Apart from all the measures described in which we can enact this, I mean *how* do we do this? What is it that gives belief in this system, why does it work, when it does? From my own life experience, which is varied, I have worked out something, and the something I have worked out might well come within the confines of modern day science as well as mysticism.

It is this. Nothing in our world is real. There is no immutable present, no unalterable situation, no buildings, no roads, no everlasting politics, all of these things are ideas and ideas can change and ideas are in our heads. At one level we all experience the same things, so, you say, how can this be? Even some of these modern day thinkers whom I have listened to, with interest, they all say, of course there are immutable laws in the universe, such as gravity. Well, there aren't. Even gravity doesn't exist, everything is an illusion, everything is created, everything changes and everything is the result of one of us somewhere creating something and the rest of us adopting it and believing in it, often without understanding it. It works therefore it is. But it only appears to exist, it only seems to be immutable, even gravity, even gravity, does not in truth exist. We can get out of it. Yes, we generally don't, but it is possible, it does happen. It has happened to me.

Democritus was a Greek philosopher who was fairly up to date in his thinking around this. He lived around 460 BC and we have little of his writings, but he is said to have believed/written/taught that the universe began with atoms and a vacuum and that everything else "*existed only in opinion.*"

This is astonishingly up-to-date at a time when microscopes hadn't been invented. Today we study and research atoms, their inter-connectivity at distance. The Hadron Collider studies particles, which are a component part of atoms, only smaller. They can exist independently of atoms as well. So Democritus could fit in well at Geneva or its environs. The important thing, for us here, is that he stated early on that everything existed only in opinion. And I would say I agree with that, everything is an idea, everything can change, nothing is permanent, everything is an opinion.

Where does that leave us? Well, it leaves us as creators believing, steadfastly, in our own creation. And this belief does not always work to our advantage. Revenge, hatred, jealousy are belief systems that appear justified and often result in action, but they are not inherently good ways of using our creative power. And then there is spirit, and where does it fit in in a world where you say we create our own reality *entirely* and that nothing is real?

It's a huge responsibility and yet effortless at the same time, for we do create. If we create only in order to have then we may get, and many New Age teachers focus on achieving material success, but they also focus on spirit, which they may call the universe, a source of spiritual fulfilment and support. So it's not entirely material oriented, which is fine if you're of a religious bent, as material achievements do not have much merit under this belief structure, which is summarised very nicely by Ecclesiastes where it says that material accomplishments by themselves do not amount to very much – "*all is vanity and a striving after wind*". This is so beautifully said, Ecclesiastes 2:11 if you want to pursue it further. A striving after wind, something you cannot hold and cannot contain. So New Age teachers are not recommending you only go after material possessions, though you can if you want to, they tell you to rely on a universal source which will support you in achieving anything you want to.

And that universal source has to be a mixture, a mixture of ourselves and a spiritual source outside ourselves, from which we come and to which we return. We ourselves are a part of everything, including creation. We create, spirit creates and to the extent to which we go along with spirit we create better and faster, but we all create and everything we create appears to us to be good - and real. This is where we fall down, because it's not real and that very fact is the reason we can and do draw things to us that we want. We imagine, we dwell in thought, we believe, we act and we have. What we wish for suddenly appears in front of us, especially and all the more so if we have relinquished all thoughts of having to have that particular thing and trust in spirit (essentially our own power backed up by what may be spiritually right for us) to deliver. And it does, it delivers on all belief systems, just sometimes our underlying belief system is that we truly don't deserve and why should that good thing happen to *us* which rather holds us back.

You'll notice I give spirit equal billing. In truth, spirit comes first by a long way, but we are creatures of spirit, from spirit we come, to spirit we return, and if we truly think about that and take it on board it backs us up in our beliefs that what we most desire we a) do deserve and b) is coming to us. Have you noticed how often vision boards take effect without our being aware of it. These are boards or walls where we post pictures and words of what we want to happen, our dearest and most meaningful desires at the point in time when we post them. We take our attention off them, notice them without being aware as we've positioned them, as suggested, in a place of maximum visibility, and then sometime later we look again and think – to our amazement perhaps – oh, I've already got that or I've had that holiday and it was exactly as imagined, or I have that wonderful house and my goodness it looks exactly like that picture I put up there, even to the colour of the door. So we've impregnated our unconsciousness, because unconsciously we'll still be dwelling on our wants, and it has gone into action to produce in our lives what we truly wish for and what we expect. It's a sort of genie, you rub the lamp by putting up pictures then you relax and trust in the genie to deliver. You don't second guess the genie by going to another genie and another. You rest on your confidence and relax and relaxation may be one of the keys to success. You achieve so much more easily when you're not too stressed out by the outcome.

In some situations this is known as confidence. Imagine two speakers, one of whom knows he is a great speaker and is entirely at ease in front of an audience and the other who is lacking in confidence and not at all sure he will deliver. Who will give the better speech ? Who will have the confidence necessary to relax and perhaps bring in a touch of humour and not belabour his message too much. Which of these will interact better with the audience, because you need a level of confidence to do that? If you can convince yourself you'll give a good speech, you're all the more likely to do that. This is what the New Age industry is based on.

And not just the New Age industry. Inspirational thinkers and actors from different times, such as Mahatma Gandhi, who said this:

"Your beliefs become your thoughts, your thoughts become your words, your words become your actions, your actions become your habits, your habits become your values, your values become your destiny".

If none of it is real, why do you say that and how can you even prove it?

27. Terror and Psychosis

From first principles in that something happened in my own life that went against the so-called immutable laws of nature and I may come onto that later. I've written about it elsewhere and it always seems forced to talk about it because it mattered so much, it hasn't happened since and, finally, no-one comes even close to believing it. And yet it happened. It happened when I was in prey to paranoid psychosis and following the instructions I received from spirit to the letter, something I later ceased to do, for practical reasons but nonetheless it saddens me because I think and feel I should have continued. At that time I lived with the abject terror of paranoid psychosis for fourteen years and I prayed to spirit every moment of every day. It was the only certainty that brought me through the fear of death in many different ways. I knew always that spirit would be there no matter what happened to me in the real world, and believe me my imaginings were not something you would choose to live with. I lived through that time with the awareness that even if I were killed, which I firmly believed was on the cards, my eternal life would continue with spirit and I knew spirit would be there and continue to support. So I was in a state of constant prayer as well as constant terror for a very long time and when that period of time ended, as most things do, the relief of not living in terror was incredible, and I noticed that lightness of being very much. So terrorised was I that I couldn't turn my head because of the physical tension I was under and at one stage I couldn't eat or speak. I got through this because I was self-employed, so there was no-one to remark that perhaps I didn't seem totally myself ! I was also very self-contained, independent and, being reliant on a self-employed income, I couldn't go to anyone for help, because the medical way out, which is the wrong way I feel, is very obvious. To me this was a spiritual journey, one I had embarked on much earlier and to them it was simply a misfire on various fronts, to be medicated but not investigated. Not one medic asked my life history, had I taken drugs, no, where there situations of stress in my life, no, it was purely a medical problem to be cured by medication. Therein lies half the problem with modern living, we are not allowed to have spiritual experiences if they upset our equilibrium, perish the thought we could exist without being medicated. Drug companies have a long reach, but that shouldn't concern us here because there are ways through and spirit is a much more powerful and effective companion than a drug company, no matter their sphere of influence.

So there I was, and as I say, I may tell you what happened later on in this book, depending on how we go. Actually, I think I may already have described it, but there's no harm in mentioning it again.

So, if everything is illusion, why do we meet with the same experiences and are these experiences totally within our grasp or are some of them perhaps pre-ordained by spirit or agreed by ourselves when we were previously in spirit and therefore not easily altered? Have we agreed to meet some situations and if that's so, is it at all possible for us to remove ourselves totally from these agreed mindsets, which in turn equate to encounters and events met and struggled with in life? For you'll agree that some people appear to have an easier ride in life than others.

28. Astrology Does Work–I Know, but Bear with

Here is where we go woo woo, because I'd like you to consider that astrology might work. I'll offer some qualification here, as I've been involved in astrology for over 50 years and have an established and highly considered qualification in it. So I'd be biased, but my bias comes from all those years of experience. It doesn't work well, in the sense that it's difficult to predict with any certitude definite events or experiences, rather it works in terms of the *type* of experience you might meet and the *timing* for these experiences. I would also say, which is blindingly obvious of course, that we improve our chances the longer we live, as experience is a great teacher, and if we truly foul up in certain areas of life we most probably will alter our approaches, and ergo alter the outcomes, at least to a degree. So we improve and it's likely we can get rid of our bad patches altogether.

But it does work and I've thought a lot about *why* it might work, because sceptics dismiss it out of hand as being improbable and just another con job, where you can say almost anything and people will accept it, as people tend to do. Think for a moment of the psychological test where a room of people were given a personal reading and most of them rated it as being correct. Not all though, there's hope, as the given reading was the same for all of them. So it is with astrology. If you word it blandly enough the listener will accept and agree, all the moreso if you're doing a personalised reading, as the client has a vested interest in believing that this will help. So you can be as indefinite as you like and still have a degree of success. And at times you can be resoundingly accurate, some astrologers more than others, and this all takes considerable work and research.

It is a craft that works and, to my mind, is one of the most helpful of disciplines in understanding how your life works, when it works, and in giving a wider spiritual view of life that religions do offer, but they do so on faith. Astrology needs no faith, no trust, if it works you'll see it and it can be of enormous value.

Now why it works is another matter. Clearly it's been researched for many centuries, times when computers were not around, when astronomers, as astrologers were then, had to go out and view the night skies through a variety of handheld instruments, make copious notes and do so night after night. They then had to study the effects of such planetary movements on people, so naturally this took time and intelligence, because a degree of mathematical genius was required, and, times being what they were, astrology was the expensive preserve of a few, namely rulers of kingdoms to start with. It could be precarious. It is said that Tiberius, a Roman Emperor 1BC, almost threw his astrologer Thrasyllus off a cliff before Thrasyllus correctly predicted that Tiberius would return to Rome. Nothing succeeds like success. He must have been sweating a lot. Nowadays there's no such danger attached, but astrologers do get mocked. So it was an elite study, and still requires mathematical skill and precision, and dare I say it intuition.

So one of the first thing any earlier astrologer would have noticed is that the Moon tends to have an effect on human behaviour. The Moon is relatively close to us, and clearly affects the tides, ebb and flow, with the Full Moon tending to correlate with more noticeable effects, such as in increase in the birth rate at that time or an increase in violent or erratic behaviour. This could be demonstrated and can be explained by the Moon's proximity. It pulls on our inner being, which mainly consists of water. It's not easy to believe that the other planets work in similar fashion, as they are all far too far away to have a sort of radiating presence. So what is going on?

Astrologers tend to explain that synchronicity is at work, that what is of the moment holds sway across multiple disciplines, the planets shadow behaviour on earth, they symbolise certain movements in time, and hence they correlate with behaviours or events. This synchronicity works across all levels, personal, geographic, geopolitical, rises and falls in empires, in fashion, all can be predicted by correctly interpreting upcoming movements of outer planets in particular. So if you want to be favoured in any endeavour, choose one that ties in with upcoming planetary phases because what is foretold will be the flavour of the month or generation and tuning into that makes sound professional or personal sense. People do this, of course, without a knowledge of astrology, because the cosmos tends to seed ideas that can be picked up by several different people in different places at the same time, hence battles over copyright ideas and so on. What is due to come in does come in, through those who are most open to ideas coming into the mainstream.

29. Did We Invent Astrology

I'm not done with astrology yet, as I'm not suggesting that the missing link to life is having your chart done. It can be highly beneficial, especially for children, but that's not the idea I wish to get across here. I've thought about why it works in the great expanse of things. And here I have to say that I think we may have invented it. I've been arguing that nothing in life is real, that we live in a spiritual reality where we are creators. I don't believe astrology was handed down to us on a tablet, so we've worked at it through research, we've built it up and today too we continue to do that, as dwarf planets are discovered and incorporated, and more and more side effects to astrology, minutiae, are poured over and interpreted. We interpret them and somehow they start to work. Perhaps their meaning corresponds to the timing of their discovery, perhaps they are symbolically linked to the moment of first discovery, the patterns inherent in the universe just then, just as nations can be charted from the timing of their inception, as can companies, and there is value in doing so as these, what are called mundane charts, can be very accurate indeed. Almost as if a company or country had less say in its own development than an individual does.

In a world where nothing is real and nothing is solid, we can create. It's easier to create into a void, than into certainty. In a solid world there are solid counterbalances and obstacles we perceive that may work in a real fashion and we believe this and so hold back on our endeavours because we believe, believe, that there are reasons why we should not succeed. We have created everything around us, everything in the material world we see has come from a source of imagination or inspiration being developed and worked upon, with belief and continuity. Someone believed in light, another believed in transport, some believed in air travel, in nuclear fission, in medical aid, in ship building, in fire, in building pyramids, it all originated from a thought or belief system. And astrology may be no different. We have put together a system and because we believe in it, the system works. It almost takes on a life of its own, it expands, develops and is seen to be accurate - if you've looked at it at all, and yet it's highly personalised, it's geocentric and human centric. We believe that it works and lo, it works. It truly does, you can take a child's chart, which is well worth doing, and predict the type of response and event that child will encounter, because all life paths are different, and you can predict when most troubles or most positive events will occur. Then it's up to the child to deal with these as well as he/she can, when the time throws them up, and most likely do better as he/she gets older, at which time the truly nasty aspects of any chart may fail to have much effect and the client may well say, well, I used to be that way but I'm not that way any longer.

It's all highly symbolic, to the extent that words also take effect. The naming of a planet may be happenstance, such as Pluto which was discovered at a time of upheaval, and certainly transits of Pluto to your chart, dwarf planet as it may be, can wreck havoc as, just as the God of the Underworld whom it is named after, it drags you down to the depths, it destroys your previous life and it returns you to the upper world utterly changed, as you may survive with a different, enhanced understanding, but you never forget the underworld and the havoc it created. True too that you may not survive, there is that. I find it most interesting that the name given to this planet should so much symbolise the events it creates, highly suspect if you want to hold onto the view that life is fixed and no such thing as astrology or symbology exists. You might have a hard time clinging to a prosaic view of life if you look a little closer.

Now the missing link in all of this is that we essentially create into a vacuum. Which, as I said, is so much easier, it's easier to believe you can have an effect if all of the world around us is malleable, all of it is energy, all of it is formed of particles, it can all be moulded to whatever we want and this is what many books on positive thinking fail to mention. The universe being on your side is one thing, as spirit is, the spiritual essence of things is to my mind undoubted, but the fact that reality just isn't what we see out there is rarely mentioned, it's the background to creation, the missing link that might help us create better, create more in line with spirit and the zeitgeist, because if we believe and understand that nothing exists, that all is vanity and a striving after wind, if we can assimilate that, we are so much closer to believing that our wishes, wants, desires, hopes, aspirations can more easily take shape as there is nothing, nothing to prevent them doing, save for our own doubts and disbelief. And we may be less attached to them. Because we know we live in an intangible, unreal and spiritual reality.

30. Ideas Arise at the Same Time

Nothing that we create is real either, it is all malleable, it is all time related, as at a different time and in a different place it may not have existed at all. We create in line with the zeitgeist, I've mentioned this earlier. The trends that are prevalent and coming into being at any given time, and whilst these trends can be predicted using the outer planets, such knowledge, while extremely helpful, is not necessary. Just an aside here, if you're at all doubtful about the efficacy of planetary awareness, J.P. Morgan, one of America's most successful entrepreneurs and an influential investment banker, said this. *"Anyone can be a millionaire, but to become a billionaire you need an astrologer."* However, to return to the plot, you can manage perfectly well without astrological awareness if you listen inwardly. In doing this you become aware of feelings and instincts that are, unknowingly, connected to everything else out there and so you have an epiphany or a feeling that there is something here to be done, something to be created, and you have the belief that you can be the one to do this, and so you act. You act on imagination, instinct, an inner knowing and because things of the time have the energy of that time and are striving, striving to come into effect, you may not be the only one with this awareness, you may not be the only one working to bring these ideas into existence. So we have different inventors in different places coming up with very similar ideas at the same time. Films, books, mechanical devices, building styles, anything you care to mention can be widespread in their idea, and can crop up in different countries and at the same time. The feel of expansion is everywhere.

And spirit thrives on expansion. The universe is expanding. So many of us hold back, convinced that we are not worthy, credible, good enough and so the idea takes root but someone else grabs hold of it. This is no great problem in the larger scale of things, because ideas may not much mind who brings them to fruition. It is undoubtedly a problem for you if you do not take action due to a lack of belief that you are good enough, and that is what many self-help books seek to address. They wish to alter your belief system through a variety of exercises that will change your belief system and so spur you to action, without which many positive changes fail to take effect.

But mainly they operate from a view that the world is real and that physical universal laws operate. They don't. Even the universe, large as it is, may be an illusion of sorts because everything is a striving after wind. So we take it on trust, we investigate further, and when we extend our horizons, we find, naturally, concrete proof that what we posited, what we imagined in this or that situation does indeed exist. Sometimes we find something out of place, that cannot be explained, but we still seek to fit it into our very limited sphere of awareness.

So we have an unfortunate number of people who are inclined to dismiss things as being impossible because, firstly, they have not personally encountered them and, secondly, because they were brought up believing that such and such was possible and such and such was not, and nothing in our ever present media coverage suggests otherwise. Perhaps I'm elaborating this idea because I wish to really stress that nothing, nothing out there has any real existence at all, everything is in flux, everything is a mass of atoms and everything moves in line with a prime motivator. Did I not mention this? The world of spirit, a spiritual awareness throughout that gives sense to the whole and whose intention, if there is one, may be far beyond our somewhat limited comprehension.

That can bring us onto religions, although it's not strictly necessary to go there, some reading here may be committed to one religion or another, or at least have an inherent belief in the doctrine they were taught when younger, and some doctrines are much supported by the larger world around us, such as Christianity which is much taught in western Europe and Islam which is much followed in the East. They differ, but in one essential they are the same, spirit exists, God exists and each religion has its prophets.

31. A Malleable Population

In a world where everything is spirit, we all feel at some stage in our life an urge to reconnect, a spiritual emptiness that in some way we wish to fill. Our soul cries out for an original connection and so we fill this with whatever symbols best fit our life circumstances. Stone Age man worshipped the sun and moon, Norsemen worshipped warrior gods, the mediaeval western world worshipped in a mediaeval way, religion was imbued with savage death, dying figures and all around killing and what you could call evil still persisted, through all of these stages. Some religions sought it out as a way of appeasing the gods, here we have the Aztecs and signs of ritualised killings that were sought to propitiate the gods, and in the western world we have stories of harvest sacrifice to bring about a better harvest. Religion doesn't do away with the horrific, it sometimes seeks it out. A sort of catharsis that cleanses our soul and redeems our misdeeds. It isn't necessary. We presently, more and more, connect to spirit in a different way, a less troubled way and we see it as supporting us even though we are – just saying – less than perfect. Religion is cleaning up its act in certain parts of the world, but it can still be savage, it can still exclude, it can still be partisan and it can still turn its back on any argument that might affect it in the long run.

If I say that any of us can create miracles, that will go against the prevailing view in the Catholic church, that only saints create miracles and ever more frequently saints are seen as what we might call extreme do-gooders, a domestic sort of saint who cares and whom people believe in, a symbol of goodness on a ten point scale, as long as the saint fits in with the teachings of the Catholic church or comes from a good Catholic background. This is pointless. You may obtain healing if you believe in the intercession of such a, generally dead, saint, that's entirely possible, more than possible, quite likely. But you may also obtain healing if you believe in the healing power of a four leafed shamrock, or a piece of crystal, or a fountain spring. It's the belief that does the work, and also perhaps the appeal of a pretty place, an expensive jewel, a reminder of the natural world, the symbols chosen as targets for our belief generally create in us a feeling of admiration or well-being, but they still work and they work, as I have said, because we believe in them.

We create our reality in accordance with our belief structures and with structures mainly approved by the mainstream at any time in our lives. We tend to be sheep. And in these most recent generations we are sheep being lulled into sleep and complacency by an ever-present media. This takes up time, often more time than we give to our own well-being, our own development, our own spirituality. We worship at the fireside in cosy slippers with a pack of crisps in our hands, that's often the case and it's rather a waste of time. If you want to create you need to take some action and put some thought into it, and these pasttimes stand in the way of that, as they may well be intended to do. A sheep-like population is an easier population to control.

You do not need to dwell on this, because it need in no way hold you back, but there may be a vested interest in under-educating a population if you want to impose a limited viewpoint on it, or indeed if you wish to sell a product. A malleable or medicated population that does not think for itself is not such a threat to continued supremacy, so if you're a leader with a strong mindset in one direction you may view a sentient active population as a threat, and thus take action through laws and conditioning and reliance to prevent this. This downwards trajectory is not in the best interests of humanity but never doubt that it exists, and then don't pay it much heed because your own development, your own spirituality, lie mainly in your own hands, so question, question, question and then go your own way.

Because you're worth it – and because humanity can only benefit from a thinking population that values their own spiritual development, and that of others.

Even severe social constraints need not concern you if you value your own beliefs and act in the knowledge that you are supported by spirit, each step you take forward, spirit nudges you even more. And to know that you are developing in a vacuum, a space where in truth there are no obstacles because even obstacles such as these do not in reality exist, they are all wind, they are all vain, they are an imaginary premise drawn up by someone else and you do not need at all to give them credence, or fear them.

If you live in a highly autocratic society then there may be reason to fear action, it depends how fearless you wish to be. If you want to avoid martyrdom, political or religious, it may be wise to keep your opinions to yourself, although some brave souls go against this at seminal points in their life, think Rosa Parks, Alexei Navalny, Martin Luther King, Nelson Mandela, Gandhi, there are countless others who have by their actions made the world a better or kinder place, but if we look again at even this short list, we shall see that in the main they are mostly dead. Speaking your truth can come at a price.

So do carry on as if your actions can make a difference to the unreal reality we see around us. I believe, although I have no proof for saying this, that spirit supports love and fairness more than hatred and division. We are spiritual beings in an imperfect world and our every force, our every feeling draws us to a spiritual outcome, a spiritual reality that we find in many different places, a baby's face, a countryside scene, the soaring waves, the crash of thunder, the stars at night which so many of us now don't see, these all convey a sense of the transcendent or the divine.

How does this differ from generalised New Age thinking? Purely in this, that there is no reality there to start with, it is all imaginary, it is all created. We create for many reasons and our beliefs arise from many points or experiences. But beyond our belief structures lies an impelling force that pushes us to strive towards spirituality, that leaves us feeling empty or incomplete if we don't, a spiritual reality that we wish to move towards and that sometimes we hold back on.

I am writing this book to make manifestation easier. If you can accept that the world around us is not real, then anything you wish to create can and should take place. This knowledge or awareness will make it so much easier for you believe that you can create. If we've all created everything around us, then there is little you cannot do. You can use all the techniques so well explained by the Secret and other writers, many other writers, but you will do so with an added impetus - an increased belief that it is possible for you to do it. That you too are a powerful being, equal in ability to those you are listening to on tape, video or reading in books. There is no power on earth that would hinder you, although as with the examples above, there are some powers that would stop you in your earthly tracks if they can. Some of those I mentioned lived through to prosper, some did not, making a huge difference for people can come at a cost, but all the people I mentioned made a difference and all are well remembered.

I'd prefer you to have a good and comfortable life in your search for spiritual reality and for most of us that is possible, so remember always that you are not in the grip of unconquerable forces and that sooner or later kindness or greatness of spirit generally prevails.

32. Nothing Exists

It's a hard act, isn't it, believing that something is possible for you and acting as if nothing in this world can stop you? In reality, I think, there are some things that can stop you, at least momentarily. Galileo had the right idea about the solar system but was convicted of heresy by the Catholic church, which held up his theories until they were accepted three centuries later. Meanwhile, he had a rather mild punishment for daring to think, he was put under house arrest, probably given his age at the time. Many thinkers have suffered worse and they all followed their dreams, so it is not at all a given that all will be well, but if you're working on grand thoughts there is a chance, and if you're simply working on making more money or finding a suitable spouse, well your awareness that we live in a vacuum through which you can draw in anything you want, and it do no ill, will definitely speed up the entire process for you. It's an added extra and it isn't much, if at all, mentioned in anything I've read. I haven't studied Eastern sages who might well dwell on this, but in the western think industry as it presently is, I haven't come across anyone who's actually said nothing around us exists. They talk of spirit, positive thinking, drawing things to you through belief, the universe, the procedures to follow, the fact that belief is what brings about success, all of this which is fine, but they don't go further and say that we live in a world that we have created, that it is not stable, it is malleable, the atoms and protons which make it up are in continual movement and continuously communicate with one another, so it's no great thing for an atom in America to send out a message to one in Australia, for instance, to bring you, by post or otherwise, what you're most looking for. The world is set up to advance you, it is set up to obey your believed commands, it will support you, it will bring positive things to you and it is, above all else, interested in your spiritual progress. It's maybe not so interested in a good bank balance, but if that's what you want, well, hey, maybe progress at creation will lead you to think more deeply about life and maybe then you'll get beyond possession and onto spiritual ideas.

You'll notice I said "do no ill" and have touched on that before. You cannot draw to yourself something that is not yours. You cannot put out for the wife who is presently married to someone else, it just won't work. You cannot envy the other the money they have or complain about their social position. What they have has nothing at all to do with what you can draw to you and if, by chance, you did manage to draw a separating wife to you, it might well not work out terribly well. Karma is a colossal bitch, it may be that someone in later years views your then wife favourably and decides to draw her to himself, and might well win. That's not a good look and not something to go looking for. Envy, contempt, scorn, sarcasm simply do not work in this world we are entering into. Appreciation for what the other person has, admiration for their gifts, even just letting them be as they are are better options and will serve you better. This is not new, most New Age writers dwell on this sooner or later, so when you decide what it is you wish to manifest, think during this process about those words "and it do no ill" and let it inform your decisions. It is important as the universe appears to be beneficial, plants respond well to good thoughts, badly to others, water crystals are beautifully cohesive and shaped when beamed at positively, but fragment horribly when the thoughts are of destruction or hatred. I know a lot of this is familiar to you and I am writing because of personal experience, I'm not simply writing out of a well-thought out dogma or belief system, I've lived through life with a constant connection to spirit, and a prayerful attitude to spirit through some of the toughest of times.

Having said that, I'd like to come onto how our brain operates, because it isn't the only intelligence in our body. We think it is but there are instances of people with very few brain cells managing to do things, achieve things, attain things that should be well-nigh impossible for them, given the lacking parts of the brain. This could happen by accident or at birth and sometimes these missing cells start to recreate, at least in part, so many things are possible. But the brain is not the only intelligence. Let me give you a personal experience that startled me greatly at the time. I had separated from a dearly loved partner and missed him greatly. Years later we met up again and I went to say hello, we'd agreed to go for a drink. So I was going to stand there, say hello and then move off together. To my utter surprise my body moved forward to be much closer to him. I had in no way given it any instruction to move forward, the opposite if anything was the case. I wasn't moving from any subconscious thought or inspiration, this was something entirely new to me. My body simply moved forward by itself, it held a residual memory of being close that had nothing to do with my brain, and this action totally surprised me.

Nurses, when we die, sometimes say they see the spirit leaving, coming out above the body and perhaps floating through an open window, and sometimes they are said to leave a window open so that the spirit can leave. I think the spirit may, in some cases, hang around a while. I'm not sure it leaves right away. I've seen a few bodies. In my father's case there was something of him still left there, in my mother's case there was nothing of her left at all, she simply wasn't there. There was a difference. Given that I believe that the body has a separate intelligence from the brain, and that I suppose (because I clearly do not know for sure) that the spirit may linger for a little while, in my own life I am against organ donation from the newly deceased. I am aware of all the arguments in favour, I just don't personally agree with them. It may be that the rapid harvesting of organs can leave an indelible imprint on the spirit or soul, which may still be around somewhere. My reaction is, I suppose, something like that of Victorian people who feared being buried alive and so arranged for a bell to be available to them inside the grave, one they could ring if they came to again. My reaction is something like that. I do not want to cause trauma to my residual spirit or soul and if that is selfish, so be it. I'm not saying this will be the truth for anyone else, I'm not suggesting it as an approach, but given that I firmly believe intelligence resides elsewhere in the body than simply in the brain, and that it may not die at the same time as the physical body, then I'm personally taking no risks. I nourish my spirit in different ways and if my body has a separate thinking function to my brain, well then I'm doubly blessed and have intelligence and information coming in from various sources and not just from one. So if you get too caught up with your own intelligence and think things out to the point of exhaustion, relax, your body is on the job and there's nothing much you can do to improve on its awareness. Except, of course, take good care of it - which you do, don't you ?

So it's a multi-faceted universe, even in areas where you think it couldn't possibly be.

33. The Path You Choose for Yourself

I would like to point out that the path you choose for yourself is closely aligned to your talents and your innate understanding of the way your life should go. So if you're wondering which path to go down in terms of manifestation, what do you do to achieve your dream, what should your dream even be, then find the things that give you joy, that you enjoy doing because these things will almost certainly be connected to abilities you have that someone else may not have, and that you may not even be seeing. Some people do, on occasion, long to be something for which they have absolutely no talent, but I would think this is somewhat rare. I'm thinking of one example here, Florence Foster Jenkins, who lived in C19th America and who wanted so, so much to be a soprano. She had a great deal of success for perhaps the wrong reasons and she became a society must see. She was a terrible singer. I have no qualms in quoting the poet William Meredith, whom I have to confess I'd never heard of, oh God he was Poet Laureate, just shows what I know. But I am better informed about New Age writers, I don't know whether that's a recommendation or not, anyway he wrote that a Florence Jenkins' recital "*was never exactly an aesthetic experience, or only to the degree that an early Christian among the lions provided aesthetic experience; it was chiefly immolatory, and Madame Jenkins was always eaten, in the end.*" Lovely, isn't it, he had a great grasp of language. Perhaps Florence had had a previous existence as an opera singer and harkened back, but we have no way of knowing. She achieved fame and affection, and well attended concerts. But she is somewhat of an exception, as most of us harken to do something we intuit or already know we are good at. We follow our passions because that's what they are, we get lost in them, we enjoy doing them, we happily spend hours exploring them and so, if we focus on these when goal setting, as we tend to do, there is every chance that we will be successful because we're prepared to put the time in and enjoy doing so.

Not everyone has the same set of skills, self-explanatory. You choose what you love doing and so the universe reaches out to meet you halfway, because what you are good at is probably part of your intended life path, and once you set out on it, it tends to be on an upwards trajectory. So when you set yourself on a path, you are generally choosing from an already existing set of skills or interests.

You do this from experience or by feel and to a degree this is not entirely in your own hands or your own choice. Life draws us to what we are meant to do, the paths we are intended to tread and this is not entirely you choosing for yourself– rather, the universe has got there first and you are now deciding to go along with it, and so you have enormous force behind you in this choice because you are fulfilling something you are really meant to do. If you don't get to this, you may feel a little dissatisfied by life, something of a square peg in a round hole, so I encourage you to explore what you want to do – to find the path and focus you can set that is best for you and your abilities.

These are, to a degree, set in advance. You may think you've made choices that have led you to this point, and you have, you have. But at least part of your life's path may be set beforehand, you may even have agreed it before you came in. If you don't agree with that, that's fine, but as babies we already have a good part of our life path written in with us. Our life skills and paths *are* written beforehand, long before anything like good or bad parenting gets in the way and then it's up to us to decide how we go about things, how to react, so there *is* a sort of set outline. As I think I said earlier, we may in living get round some of our disadvantages until they no longer bother or hinder us, we react with experience, and the paths we tread will differ as we age. They may get higher. We may leave behind some automatic responses and as a result meet different likely outcomes, not everything is set in stone. I found it interesting, as an astrologer, comparing the charts of Mafia gangsters and anti-Mafia judges in Sicily. Their charts were very similar, they had the same themes, just that one faction had opted to be criminals and the other faction had opted to fight criminals. The themes underlying their lives were in large part the same, sometimes tragic and here I'm thinking of Judge Giovanni Falcone, whose death in 1992 still affects me. At that time I was involved in translating court documents to do with Italian corruption, so it was a very close in thing, as I think it would be for many people in Italy and elsewhere. So what I'm saying here, that is relevant to the New Age and positive thinking, is that a little celestial blackboard does exist. Why it does, how it operates is something we don't know or can't be sure of, but there are guidelines, so there is a likelihood of how we operate in life that we can work with or against. Up or down, sideways perhaps on a couch with a packet of crisps, you get the idea.

I'm suggesting that you will instinctively know the path for your life by listening to your own instincts, your interests and, yes, your passions because they will be linked to any outlined life you may or may not have. You're not interested in a particular subject by chance, your soul knows that you may be talented in that way, that you may have something to teach or to learn in that direction and so it sends you down that path and all will be well. It may take ages or it may not - time involved may be a distraction, as time ultimately doesn't really exist and success can come in an instant if you're really tuned in, or you may learn things from repeated failure.

Abraham Maslow, a well-known psychologist from the 40s, said this: "*If you deliberately plan to be less than you are capable of being, then I warn you that you'll be deeply unhappy for the rest of your life.*" He is saying that we should focus on our own potentiality and interests, as otherwise we will lead a life of non-fulfilment or lack of purpose. It may be possible to lead a reasonable life if we ignore our true passions and abilities, but it will be one without a very deep sense of fulfilment. This essentially goes back to the biblical story of burying our talents in the ground, a talent here being also a piece of money - they don't incur interest in the ground. They need to be used.

34. There is a Path Set for You

Here I'd like to look a little more at the inbred nature of things, as I've mentioned above. As an astrologer, I'd like focus a little on that because it informs me and forms a large part of who I am and of my belief system, though not entirely as we shall see. Nothing in life has given me a greater understanding of myself or other people or how we interact together. It is one of my life passions. I would repeat again that astrology is real, and it is quite worth your while having a chart done, but it is not essential by any means. If you follow your instincts, you'll possibly avoid quite a lot of negatives that might arise, as we all have positives and negatives in our chart and it's disheartening to learn we might have come into a life of great turmoil, not that anyone will ever couch it in those terms. It is of interest, though, that these difficult lives can be the most productive ones, in that struggling against our own worst traits can lead to success, we win through, whereas someone with a very easy chart, and they do exist, might not be inclined to do much in life and just sit on their many laurels. They'll still have a nice life, but without a bit of stress, a few hard angles to push them into action and into adverse events, they might miss out on a lot of what they could achieve if they pushed a little more here and there. That thought may be of some benefit.

Yes, your abilities are outlined from the start, there is an outline of a plan, and now, if you're sceptical, as many are, you might ask yourself where did it come from. Was there a sort of astrological Moses who went up to a height and came down with a nice package of inscribed tablets? Well, clearly, no. Astrology was incredibly difficult for early astrologers, as they had to be out there at all hours with an astrolabe and in all weathers, studying the sky. Maybe on a cloudy night you could take the night off, but it was an endless cycle of study, note taking, comparison and then marking possible effects in those around you. It was also mathematical - still is, although computers can take the work out of it - so early astrologers were skilled and busy and sought after only by those who could afford their counsel - namely kings and rulers, which is always a dodgy client base to work to, as I think I mentioned earlier.

So astrology arose because of noticing and noting the sky around us and then relating what we found to humans on the planet earth, because we couldn't really relate it to anyone else. As our ability to chart the heavens increased, so we found outer planets and then dwarf planets and we linked those to life on earth and drew conclusions, fairly well researched ones, and our conclusions worked - at least in part, for these outer planets can have very demonstrable effects on our lives and anyone who has lived through a Pluto transit or a Uranus transit will know that their lives became intolerably disrupted for a while or they went through sudden and unexpected changes - all of which, hopefully, came at the right time for them because they were due to rise to a different level, a sort of phoenix reborn from the ashes or a traveller settling in a strange and foreign land.

Many years ago I found a quote which I can no longer find, but I remember it in part. It said "*before grace astrology is real, after it the astrologers are no longer right*", something like that because it's many years since I noted it. I liked it because it said quite a lot to me. It said that grace, a spiritual awakening, an awareness of spirit, could undo the effects of astrology, that spirit overruled all and that if you act with spiritual awareness you would avoid many of the drawbacks of any chart. That, I think, is true. If we think of any spiritual leaders, they act from compassion, awareness, lack of fear and while their own personal outcome may not be great, many are assassinated, their chart ceased to hold them back or prevent their becoming an icon for many and a source of awakening for others.

So why am I bothering about astrology in a book which is intended to reveal the missing link in New Age thinking, because it's clearly not astrology. It is this. I think we may have created astrology. I don't think that its many different rules and readings have been passed to us by some mystic hand, I'm not at all sure that it was written in the heavens beforehand and we've discovered and embellished it as the years go by, I have a feeling it didn't exist. Many sceptics may say it still doesn't! This is outlandish, I know, but look at it this way. I am arguing that we are enormous creators and that we create into a void or vacuum that is made up of atoms and protons and New Age thinkers argue that the universe is eager to fulfil our every wish if we just get on with it and visualise and take action, which is more or less saying that these atoms and protons will respond favourably to our every demand. We are much more skilled creators than we realise, and I think it possible - only possible, mind - that we created and developed astrology from a set of observations, we created a doctrine or philosophy or way of thinking, call it what you will, that said in this circumstance such and such happens. We crafted our craft and still do. And we developed a skill set, a way of thinking, that works – just take my word for it if you're in doubt here, to a certain degree, which is all we need really, it works. Nothing works 100% so allow for lack of absolutism. We set up a system which then took on a life of its own, it progressed, much as computers may one day take over the world, it set off and hasn't stopped operating. I know that is hypothesis and you may think it highly unlikely, but I can't think of any other way that it operates.

It is mind-blowing that a planet we named Pluto should so closely correspond to life and death situations, to times of in-depth turmoil and delving into things to ultimately return to earth renewed, reshaped and able to meet a different level of future life. It is resoundingly difficult to accept that a planet named Uranus should so closely fit with times of upheaval, earthquakes and totally unexpected shocks in the way that it does. Uranus is the only planet that operates immediately. Up it comes and things go from left to right instantly. It simply doesn't make sense, unless to some extent we are doing it ourselves. We speak and it becomes so. I know that's biblical, and I have no intention of detracting from God here, in the beginning was the word and the word was with God, but we ourselves are part of spirituality and we do create. We are enormous creators, look at what we've done to date. We do use all our brain, apparently, even when we sleep, so bang goes the theory that we only use ten per cent, but there will/may be functions we haven't even tapped into yet. I'm aware of the argument of synchronicity and accept this as quite valid, that we are all one, and everything both inner and outer is linked and operates at the same frequency that is in play at any given time. What is of the moment contains within it the essence of the moment. So a planet will mirror what happens to you or to some government or in an environmental sense. Uranus can wreck havoc here. You may not agree, that's fine, you may think this a flight of fancy, but I still think we may have created astrology.

Words are important and naming something seems to give it a life of its own. Past generations spent time on numbering the alphabet to estimate the life path of a person's name. They believed that the name given had some influence over development. In horseracing it is sometimes possible to guess the outcome of a given race by comparing the names of the horses with the prevailing astrological trends at the time of the race, so they may have had something there. You can study form along with that, because a 33/1 outsider even with a great name for the day has not a great chance of winning, but nonetheless it can be done. Personally I've found it works best with large national races with many horses competing, and even then only if you can find a horse that corresponds to the aspects. For me it doesn't work so well with smaller races. Sometimes you will find several horses with a close similarity and in that case your goose is cooked, unless you're prepared to place an each way bet on each of them and in a large race this may be feasible. (As the odds are good, for those of you who don't follow horseracing). This doesn't make sense either, does it? It might lead you to suppose that it's a very strange world, where a horse's name might make it a winner in certain circumstances. And it is a strange world indeed, it's strange because it simply isn't what it appears to be, and this is greatly to your advantage if you wish to exploit positive thinking or improve your own position. Even for the most mundane of reasons, more money, a better sex life, you can use this awareness to boost your efforts at visualisation and believe that what you're trying to bring about is possible, because it is possible and it's possible because the world around us consists of atoms and protons, all in constant motion, all ready to do our bidding if we can simply exert ourselves a little in the right direction.

So New Age suggestions do work out and it should benefit us to follow them, they just don't generally say that nothing of what we achieve actually exists.

35. What Not To Do

Here much of what I'm saying is straight out of the New Age handbook, but it bears reminding. The first thing is do not expect things to be handed to you on a plate. You really do need to think about what you want, visualise and take some sort of action to further your dream. This may come to you as intuition or you may simply have to sit down and work it out, but specific things that you desire to come to pass do require some sort of effort on your part and if you can enthuse yourself about your desires, such action or, dare I say, work should not be too troublesome. Think, see and act, that's the advice here. For instance, when younger I was enticed by languages, astrology and mediumship. I did in time become an excellent translator, a good astrologer and a reasonable medium in the sense that spirit talks to me and instructions sometimes come through. I spent years studying languages and years studying astrology, so it didn't just fall into my lap, but I did all of that because I was truly interested in these areas of life and wanted to progress. With mediumship I also followed a spiritual path for years, and still do, going to lectures, seminars, workshops, courses and everything I could fit in or afford. Some of it, I know, paid off in life, other parts were purely for interest. Sometimes you have to look at something in depth before you can disregard it – as possibly working for others but not for you yourself at this time. So the action here was enjoyed, but at times did equate to hard work.

The second thing to avoid is to get depressed when nothing happens. If you've done all the work and not stressed too much, that is when you can sit back for a while from all this effort and rely on something coming your way in due course. If it doesn't then maybe spirit has a different and better intention for you, but generally it should. There is an old Irish saying here "*what's for you won't pass you*" and I think this is total nonsense and quite dangerous a viewpoint because it suggests that your good will come your way whether you act or not. It's offered as a support to those who have lost someone, perhaps a young girl missing her first love, but it is nonsense and may encourage the young girl not to take any necessary action, such as going to dances or that sort of thing. It's folk advice and not great at any level. So do continue with a belief that what is right for you will come your way, but only after you have put out to the universe, through visualisation, action and prayer. Don't kill yourself in other words, either through too much action or by throwing yourself off a pier, just relax and accept that most likely something good is coming your way, because you've seeded it onto your life path. Accept too that there are people whose good comes to them without any effort at all. Some are just born lucky and that should be absolutely fine to you and you should appreciate their good fortune, because that means that you can be lucky too, try anyway.

The third thing not to do is to talk to others about what your intentions are. Sure you can tell them something like I'm going to train to become a physiotherapist, that should be absolutely fine, just don't tell them of your dearly held ambitions. I'm going to climb Everest, I think I can write a best seller, I'm going to go on a Caribbean cruise, unless you've booked it already. If you're putting out for something you dearly wish for, it may be that it appears far out of your reach, certainly it might to others. You will have reached a stage where you believe it possible and see it in all its glory coming your way, but you need faith to work magic, and others may not be compliant. Especially if they know you well. Many will be inclined to say or think - and their thoughts may be audible to you - what you, you can't possibly afford that, yeah, likely isn't it, aren't you biting off more than you can chew, oh cruise passengers get ill all the time. Keep your dearly held visions and intentions to yourself, or possibly share them with someone else on a spiritual path if you really find it impossible not to talk about such exciting events coming up, but in general keep your own counsel. Contrary advice or adverse reaction can throw us off our path. Your best route is to work with spirit, share with spirit and trust in spirit, then relax because spirit has your back and will certainly never tell you you can't achieve that. If it doesn't bring what you wish for, then just possibly it isn't for you and accepting that might bring you onto something that is right for you. In trying for what hasn't come in, you may learn something about how to proceed, actions to take that might benefit you in your next endeavour. There may be a reason for things that we just don't see. Do not lose positivity.

36. Being Part of the Whole

So far so good on the I am a creator concept. But do you remember that scene in a James Bond movie where Boris Ivanovich Grischenko, a Russian computer technician on the villainous side of things, raised his hands to heaven in joy and shouted out *"I am eenvincible"* and then was blasted to death with liquid nitrogen as the canisters behind him exploded? It's one of those unforgettable scenes where pride comes before a fall. He was a rather charismatic, if nasty, piece of work. And, of course, if we want to be strictly literal, he didn't fall, he was frozen into place in an upright and jubilant position. Such is life and naturally none of us has the chutzpah of Boris, although a degree of self-worth and self-vindication is always helpful. Be that as it may, we are creators, but we don't want to be haughty creators, blind to the fact that in the amazing greatness of things we are truly small fish. When you look at the universe and think about creation, we're an amazing outcome, we have great capacity, but it's not hard to imagine something or something that is greater than us, much greater perhaps and which may, at some time, have its hand on the liquid nitrogen canisters. Incoming, ouch.

The greater presence to which we are all subject is creation itself, the creator, spirit, the universe, God, call it what you will, it is there, it does exist and it does exert an influence. It reacts best when our intentions are, if not pure because that's a hard level to reach, at least not too biased with self-interest, thinking of helping others in our quest for glory, using compassion in our business dealings, opting not to go for other peoples' things, choosing always to act in line with a merciful God, a compassionate God, an all-encompassing God, a spiritual reality that it unknown to us, except in part, a spiritual universe of which we are a pulsating, conscious part, but perhaps a small part in the universal scheme of things. We do not have the full story, we can only believe and embellish that part that we do know and do our best to live within certain guidelines.

"For now we see through a glass darkly, but then face to face".

I Corinthians

So we are a mixture of supreme creators, in touch with universal strengths and supported by a compassionate universe, and we are still small fish and sometimes that dichotomy may hold us back. How many of us have grand thoughts and ambitions only to hold ourselves back by thinking who am I in the greater scheme of things, why should anyone listen to me, what have I to offer. And New Age thought realises this and tries to bring us beyond our limitations through a variety of exercises and encouragement. We are indeed small fry, but it behoves us to try to be massive whales, swimming the ocean surrounded by smaller fish. We need only believe that we are supported by spirit in all of this and then listen to what comes through to us, because it comes from a very safe and secure place and what we do, when we listen, may benefit not only ourselves but all mankind. Just saying. And having said that we are small fish, disregard that, for we are all also spiritual creatures, we come from spirit and to spirit we return, we are part of spirit and supported by it and, yes, we are massive, incredible creators.

37. Death, Suffering and So On

Sometimes we wonder why there is so much suffering in the world if everything's as easy as the New Age suggests, or why you, as a single person, should have suffered this illness or that accident. If you live close to spirit and listen for any suggestions coming through, there is a chance that you will have avoided many of the mishaps of life that go around, you need not fall ill, you can avoid accidents but if these have happened to you, a positive outcome and a faith in a happy outcome may help you heal faster and overcome any of the disasters that have happened. Sometimes things that have happened don't heal, but your faith or positive approach can only help you at whatever stage you're at and be a positive healing influence on those around you.

All of this happens for various reasons, things do happen, maybe you let your energy drop for a while, maybe you gave up on a healthy diet and didn't give up on smoking. These decisions are hard and require work and maybe you just felt a bit lazy. It's just the likely outcome of continuing to do what you're doing or not doing what would be recommended if you wanted a fairly disease free life. And sometimes things just happen, it may indeed just be your time to go. I'm not a fatalist, but I think often timings are set and while they're not set in stone and can be altered, by good medication perhaps or by a caring and uplifting physician or healer, at certain times it simply may be time to leave and to go on elsewhere, as I suggest we do. Our spirit continues and may return or may leave to act on a different plane, perhaps a better place, perhaps just a different place where your spirit can learn another of life's experiences on your upwards spiral through the galaxy. I believe that spirit intends us to grow and that we may be here for that purpose – it doesn't mean we shouldn't have fun while we're here. We are all connected, all part of one life force. Love, compassion, good times, everything that a happy mundane or spiritual life can offer is ours for the asking, we simply have to believe. We've forgotten the details of why we're here, but we have a sense and some sense it more than others but we can all get there.

Modern medicine sometimes may extend the life of someone who is ready to go, and who by all reasonable standards should leave. Perhaps they have little quality of life. I have no answer for this as doctors can be sued. It doesn't concern me much, but medicine that heals us may go too far at times. I've never agreed with over-medication, it can simply create another massive set of problems and arises from the viewpoint that "you're going to be ill" which is a negative approach to life. There's no way we are as ill or potentially ill as the medical profession currently suggests. We are potentially likely to die (at present) but there's nothing they can do about that and maybe death is just a part of our life's journey and we shouldn't fear it the way we do. Still it's hard to give up our life's earnings, abandon the home comforts, start again, leave behind loved people and places, we struggle against it which is natural. You'll guess I'm not in sway to the medical profession. I feel they do great harm in their reliance on statistics, drugs and a general view of the person as a machine that can be fixed and overhauled in advance of any problem. It's dehumanising. Yes, many medical people do focus on the person before them, but in some cases they have neither the time or inclination to get to know who that person is or what his personal history is, in other words they do not treat the entire person, simply a part that is malfunctioning. I didn't intend to write this and it's neither here or there. I'm saying only that we may have a time to leave and that is not necessarily a bad thing. It's awful for those remaining if it's a child or a dearly loved consort, terrible, but we may have agreed a contract beforehand knowing, unconsciously and at a spiritual level, that we would be together for a period of time, but not perhaps for ever, not perhaps for as long as we would have wished, and the parting is hard, but may be part of our life's pattern, established far in advance of the losses occurring.

I do think spirit, by its nature, is detached. Some argue "well, how can there be a God, just look at the havoc going on around us". But the havoc comes from man. The universe, which modern thinking calls it, is caring and compassionate but to a certain degree it is detached, it may not intervene and it may be working to a different agenda to those of us here on earth. We see only the human form and the human suffering, spirit sees our spiritual development, our learning, our return to source, the fact that we are all a loved part of universal consciousness, we are all connected and we all face different things, but essentially we are loved and in the bosom of a caring but dispassionate universe and in face of this, our sole solution at present, as I see it, is to focus on spiritual teachings, however we best find them, learn about positive thinking, practice meditation, listen to spirit coming through and then do our very best to focus on what we most wish for in life, to use the skills we have been given, to work in accordance with our best passions, to enjoy life, to love, to care, to give, to receive, to play, to know that we rise, for our lives are, in the smaller scheme of things, quite long with many minutes and hours to pass in wonderful ways, life is wonderful, but in the greater scheme of things and at the end may seem quite short. Such a short time, but truthfully that is a cliché and we all have a lot of time available to us to enjoy the time we have, to lead others to enjoy it and to live in a world of love and good intent. Which is certainly part of what spirit is all about. Again, we see spirit through a glass darkly, but we do intuit it.

So use your imagination to bring about the best possible life for you, to create and bring to life the images you long to create and do this with belief and joy that it is possible to bring to pass almost anything you could wish for.

Speaking of our imagination, I'd like to opt out for a second and pass the baton to other writers who have written about the world of the imagination, so here are a few quotes:

Carl Sagan, an astronomer who seems to be very quotable, says this: *"Imagination will carry us to worlds that never were, but without it, we go nowhere."*

Napoleon Hill, self-help author and one of the godfathers of the law of attraction or abundance, this: *"Imagination is the most marvellous, miraculous, inconceivably powerful force the world has ever known."*

Anatole France, a French novelist, this: "*To know is nothing at all; to imagine is everything.*"

Antoine De Saint Exupery, aviator and author of the loved fable *Le Petit Prince*, this: "*A rock pile ceases to be a rock pile the moment a single man contemplates it, bearing within him the image of a cathedral.*"

So let's get those cathedrals going because they are possible.

38. The Interface between Science and Mysticism

I think it's time to recap on what the missing bit to creative thinking is, as I sometimes go off on interesting tangents – interesting to me and I think maybe to you too – so let's come back to our original premise which is why you bought this book in the first place.

Nothing of what we see around us exists. This knowledge is shared by scientists to a degree and I'll come onto that shortly, but even to accept this in part will help your ability to manifest into your life what you most want, what you most desire and all the more so if these wishes and desires fit in with your inherent abilities or innermost feelings of where you would *most* like to go in life. If you're creating into a sentient vacuum, which is what life on earth is, then you should have an even greater ability to create and bring to you what you wish for, and it do no ill. It should and will benefit those around you and the world in general, because by the time you've reached the stage of manifesting you will likely also have reached a different level of awareness, one where the other is more or less an extension of yourself. Sure, this may not work all the time, when you're faced with someone not acting in a pleasant way, but even there your reaction may be lessened and you will, somehow, see the spirit of God in the other being. It doesn't work all the time, I accept that, sometimes you just want to retaliate and there are people from time to time who will push all your buttons, but generally you'll have got over that stage in life and onto the next, a stage where you either don't meet with these people, your life path takes you well beyond them, you're working on a different frequency, or where they affect you less – and in turn, you, by your reaction, may affect them favourably too.

So that's the big reveal – and it's, to a degree, backed up by science. That we live in a malleable world and perhaps a malleable universe, that spirit is all around and that nothing we see – nothing at all – is real or actually there. Give this approach a go as it will undoubtedly increase your ability to bring to you that which you truly desire.

On the scientific front, many scientists are still purely empirical, but some go beyond that and have theories that may – or may not – be accurate. That is in so far as accuracy goes, because sometimes what is accurate today may turn out to be only a tiny part of what is accurate in several centuries time. Things change. Michael Pravica is among the more explorative scientists. He is a professor of physics at the University of Nevada and his opinions or thoughts are not widely accepted by science but they are of interest. I should say that scientists are very interested in consciousness and how it works. He suggests that the universe is composed of more dimensions than we currently see. We have four – height, length, width and then outside of these three time. He thinks there could be more and this is a theory which is called hyperdimensionality. Scientists accept hyperdimensionality in physics, but not in consciousness. He suggests that when we dream or are highly creative our consciousness could go beyond the physical dimension and move onto a higher plane where it connects with hidden dimensions and takes from them an amazing degree of inspiration. This is equivalent to resting in the bath and shouting Eureka, is it not? It is also very close to what New Age writers suggest when they say to meditate, visualise, create, use vision boards, because in all of these we are switching off the logical part of our brain and resting in the arms of inspiration. Pravica suggests that in that state we connect with something greater than ourselves and take in a lot of inspiration that can be of value to us. While this theory is not generally accepted in the field of consciousness, it is of interest to us here because it tallies with New Age thought and because it brings us closer to a synthesis of science and magic, which can only benefit us, I think.

Then there are uncertain accounts by individuals of near-death experiences. One which has been very criticised is the account of an after-life experience by a neurosurgeon who was before that a sceptic. To quote him, as he's quite cogent here, *"what my coma journey showed me ... is that consciousness is something that is fundamental in the universe and does not originate in the brain."* He called the material world cloudy in our present state of consciousness, as if it really wasn't real. I'm not a big proponent of heaven or heavenly visions, I don't know what we'll meet. My own thinking is that it will be a sensation of joy and a melding with other energies. I don't see it in earthly terms. We all imagine it in our own ways and Dr. Alexander's account has been criticised, but I find it interesting to relate here because it echoes what I'm saying - that consciousness does not originate in the brain, just as I've argued earlier that eyesight does not originate from the eyes - yes, I did say the brain decides what we see, but eyesight is a function of the brain and here we're talking about consciousness as a whole and where it comes from.

It's the interface between science and mysticism that interests me and I think this interface is coming more into our awareness and making us realise that we are not just a set of muscles and arteries, not just a consumer to be merchandised or a sheep to be sedated, but are capable of ever greater things and a much more valid way of living our lives if we can access and believe in our capacity, which connects us to God.

39. Physics, Ouch

To go a little further into science, my knowledge of physics is close to zero and with an observer, in other words if you asked me to explain it, it would probably reduce to zero. This could be the observer effect, which can happen to all of us at one time or another as we stutter to explain our realities. If you don't suffer from this, you're ahead of the pack – and probably sitting somewhere in Geneva ! So come with me as I approach the rabbit hole for even a cursory glance. If you don't want to go there skip this bit – you won't miss much and if you're a physicist I suggest you look away now before you become too downhearted. So, with the added caveat of total ignorance, let's go .... into the rabbit hole.

Some years ago I looked at quantum physics to help with a talk I was giving. I looked at it to the extent I understood what I was reading, which meant I didn't have to spend a lot of time on it. Nonetheless, let me tell you about an experiment physicists carried out which falls within my remit – that being to persuade you that nothing around us is real and that atoms are indeed sentient, or at least communicating. *"When under observation, electrons are more or less being forced to behave like particles instead of waves. Thus, the mere act of observation affects the experimental findings."*

Scientists are at pains to point out that the observer is not always, indeed infrequently, a human being. The observers are machines and they too seem to affect the findings. So this slightly does away with the idea that human consciousness has its effect on scientific experiment, as machine observation does as well. *"The need for the "observer" to be conscious is not supported by scientific research, and has been pointed out as a misconception rooted in a poor understanding of the quantum wave function ψ and the quantum measurement process."* I don't even know what that is ! So many New Age writers start off with "quantum physics now says". Are they all geniuses ? The quote is taken from " E Scholarly Community Encyclopedia", an on-line forum with its base in Switzerland.

However you read this – or have skipped it entirely – since our universe is made up of atoms and sub-atomic particles such as protons it suggests that nothing is as solid as it seems. Come back to me here because I'd like to look at religions for a bit, which is something we all know something about.

40. Religions

This brings us onto religions, which are a thorny issue, as many of you will be over-subscribed. They originate from a basis of love and care and degenerate into wars and rules. As in any discipline there are good clerics and some not so good. Let's give religions a chance, because they will have at some stage gone with a spiritual urge to unite with something bigger than themselves and to serve spirit in whatever way they best can. Beliefs vary depending on the culture, but they mainly have this love and compassion at their heart. If it's all gone downhill from there we mainly don't look at it and it's simply a reflection of how badly things can go if pride, ambition, weariness, politicising or lack of intelligence get in the way. And if you suffer from all five you may have entered onto the wrong path in choosing religion. Why not change course and go into politics instead?

I think religions will fade out. I'm speaking here from a Western consciousness. I don't know how ingrained religions are, perhaps less ingrained in Europe, moreso in the United States and to a much greater degree in the East, so all may not change at the same time or there may be a massive shift in consciousness which would render most of them obsolete. I think over time they will fade out as we become more aware of our personal connection to all that is around us, to God. We will probably always need someone to celebrate a wedding or officiate at a funeral. Of course, you argue here, marriage itself may fade away and we may cease to die, or at least live such an extended life that being a funeral director just doesn't pay, but these are flights of fancy, entertaining and in the realms of science fiction. At present we use these rites of passage to tell the world of a vast change in our personal world and they can connect us to the divine, think of the lovely poems written to celebrate the passing of someone you love and the emotion you feel at such a ceremony. You are supported by spirit and by those around you. It helps soothe the spirit.

41. Intermission Time

After all the rather intense scientific and religious stuff, here's a quote to liven you up again. It's from Bill Watterson, who is an American cartoonist who created Calvin and Hobbes. Did I read multiple New Age writings to find this quote ? No, I noted it down from an episode of Criminal Minds because I found it so uplifting ! I suggest you check out some of his quotes, which you can find on-line, because we're here to have fun, aren't we? Here it is:

"To invent your own life's meaning is not easy but it is allowed and I think you'll be happier for the trouble."

Bill Watterson again, everyone. Someone with a lovely sense of humour. Here's another one, as we're in a bit of an intermission:

"I let my mind wander and it didn't come back."

I think that may have happened to me. Answers on a postcard, please. Now.

42. Relationships

I suppose we should go there, as New Age thought would say we can create and draw to us the person who is right for us. We need to imagine clearly what it is we want in a partner, then we visualise as much as we can the relationship we will have as if we're living it now, and we may even draw up a vision board with pictures of somebody that might fit the bill and having done all that we sit back. We don't completely relax, we just take our mind off it. In the meantime, we act as if we have a relationship, we set the table for two, I know it sounds bizarre, we make wardrobe space for another person, we lose weight if we feel we have to, we enjoy what we have right now in the certain knowledge that a well-nigh perfect relationship is coming our way. Or at least one that is liveable with for the long term. Some aren't and we don't want to duplicate that, do we ?

So, that is all fine and good and it can work and work well. It has worked well for many of the New Age pundits who seem to have drawn in perfect marriages for themselves using these techniques and others. And that is something to be very pleased about because everyone needs somebody to love. Ooh-ooh, ooh.

We don't all develop at the same rate and we don't all get to be masters of manifestation overnight. Yes, it can happen, but if it hasn't happened for you so far, or you feel you could do better, here are some thoughts. We grow as we gain experience. What works for us at one stage of life may not at another. That perfect person you thought you met might turn out to have feet of clay and you think how could you not have noticed. Attraction is a powerful force. Or you may keep meeting the same kind of experience, even though you truly don't want to draw in another alcoholic, critic, cheater, you get the picture, somehow the next one turns into just that - and you think again how could you not have noticed. You may give up at this point.

Until we've gained a degree of self-awareness and experience and certainty, we may do all of the above. Do not let this get you down and think about the following.

We may attract the person who is right for us at that time and we may learn a lot from the experience, even if it's tough. Not everyone is with us for life, not everyone is likeable when their buttons are pushed, not everyone has it in them to stay the course, and there are many alternative attractions out there. I'm not saying this to make you give up, not at all, but life is life and at times it's all too real. I believe we know in advance what we're going for when we get into a relationship. In some way the other person may draw to you a re-run of what you experienced when you were growing up. If you were highly criticised, it's all too likely you'll draw to you someone who criticises you for everything, except for the initial stages when he/she could be very laudatory. You just don't see it coming. As you grow in awareness this won't happen so much and you may have resolved something in yourself, because it's always in yourself, and you may have stopped drawing in such negativity and crisis situations. We interact in different ways with different people and we act out again the connections we had with those closest to us in our early life.

So know that your awareness and certainty and positivity will draw to you their equal in your life, someone who is also kind, resourceful, optimistic, well-balanced and so on. You really have to be the person you wish to draw to you. Because most things to do with relationships are a reflection of yourself and, when all comes to all, you do need to be at peace with the wonderful and unique person you are, because no-one, anywhere, is quite like you or has quite the set of skills and experiences that you bring to life or to the table, as they say in business. Also, sad fact though it is, no-one will be with you as long as you are.

As we think so shall it be done to us. As a man thinks, so he is.

Proverbs

So when you feel or know you are ready, draw to you the relationship that is right for you at that time, one which will benefit you both and which you can really rest in with love and compassion. Ask, believe, receive and know that you are manifesting into a vacuum.

There may be a timing element here, and relationships tend to come in when the time is right. You may know when someone is coming in, and at those times it makes sense to accept invitations and all the rest, to simply spread your net further. It may be pre-set, it may not, your psychic awareness may be great or it may not, it doesn't much matter. If you really desire to be in a relationship, put it out there, work on yourself a lot, be as certain as you can, believe and as you think, so shall it be.

I don't want to dwell on relationships too much. They are just one part of what we might want to have in our lives, money is another, foreign travel, good health, a lovely garden, a weight loss to make us ultra-desirable, a fabulous wardrobe, a front seat at a Paris catwalk, delicious food, the very best in wines, lovely jewellery, a book published, so many things that you can draw to you and imagine into your lives.

These are lovely things, they are also not the main thing. If we can draw to us peace of mind, happiness, a connection with spirit, a feeling of holiness in the depth of nature, a belief that we are not alone, a knowledge that we do not die, rest in the Holy Spirit and a depth of awareness for the other people around us, compassion and a liking for mankind, then these are truly virtues to enjoy, and having all the rest, all the above, all the pleasures of an earthly existence, does not detract from any of this. Set yourselves free, go for it all, and don't worry at all if you get too much. You can manage it !

Your instincts can be off in relationships, but follow them anyway. As you progress with New Age thought or teachings, you'll find you gain insights and feelings that you might not have taken on board earlier. Trust your gut and expect the best!

43. In Case of Doubt–Credentials

At this point you may think some of the contents of the book are so unlikely you wonder whether or not to accept them.

You may say who am I to say this is right and some of the theories or ideas I've put down may seem to you on reflection - or even immediately if you're quick to critique - outlandish, so let me tell you again why I've written it and present you, once again, with something like a credential, through from a New Age standpoint these are hard to pinpoint, as really anything much goes. I have a few credentials Here are some of them.

I have been psychic for as long as I can remember, but I didn't always know this. I have porous membranes, everything comes through. Astrologers, if they've held with me this far, may see my astrological placements as sufficient credential, although I'm not sure they'll agree with much of what I've written on astrology. I was born with Venus Neptune South Node Ascendant and Moon Mercury on the 12 house cusp. To the general reader this would indicate someone who is tuned in in some way and who is most comfortable when writing. All exact. It could indicate big time illusion, but I'm trying to convince you that what I'm saying is real.

Like many of you I can intuit a situation, sense unease, see situations developing ahead of time and, as many introverts do, I can attempt to calm situations. I generally don't bother. That's an odd thing to say, but I can be fairly detached. Where I may differ from many readers here is that I have experienced spiritual events that are not usual and which have led me to many of the beliefs that I now have, or rather have led me to believe with certainty in things that I only used to feel were true. From early days I wanted to have a greater knowing of spirituality, I wanted to become closer to God. I was drawn by mysticism and I pursued learning. I experienced coincidences and dreams.

In one of these dreams I was staying in a communal house and had a very vivid dream of a Red Indian running along a tunnel when suddenly he was struck from behind with an axe and fell. It was unusually vivid. That night in the room next to mine someone died. He was a nice man and died ahead of his time. I heard about it a day or so later. You may say, oh you heard something, but I hadn't.

I have known with absolute certainty when I was going to win a raffle. I won a large wicker basket filled with drink and food. To be honest I thought at the time of the draw that I hadn't won and was much dismayed because I'd earmarked one or two of the tickets as the winning ticket and in fact it was one of the other ones I held. I don't nit-pick so I didn't go, what, the wrong ticket won it, what are we at? I was young, I didn't have a lot and I was greatly pleased. I haven't been able to replicate that degree of certainty since, otherwise I'd have everything flowing to me.

That same week a client presented me with a large bouquet of flowers to thank me for my work. Maybe my star was just in the ascendant that week, because rarely have I had such a wonderful looking table.

I have lost connection with the everyday and entered into a different space where everything was connected. This was at an evening class celebration where everyone became one. It was a feeling of connection with an immensity and very pleasant.

I have, and here I'm not happy to say it, almost killed someone by beaming hatred at him for an entire evening. There were reasons for this and I wouldn't do it now, but it explains why I sometimes say "and it do no ill" because the mind is very forceful, both for good and for ill and when we put our whole intent behind it, when we really, really feel something, then it can take effect. That's why it's important, I feel, not to focus on other peoples' successes because that could bring envy into your life and your own successes will, of necessity, be different to theirs. You do not covet your neighbour's wife. What we need in life is faith and awareness of spirit. You can manage without the awareness of spirit, but it's better to bring that along too as it will improve your life beyond measure.

I'm trying here to offer some explanation of why you might believe some of what I've written here and I don't mean to sound over and above. We all have these abilities, we can all draw things to us, we can all affect others by our thoughts as well as by our actions and we all, all of us, have the ability to manifest. We are also much loved and supported on this path.

On the events side of things, and not just the beaming of thoughts, I've been airlifted out of a river by spirit and set on a beam above the surface of the water and this was against all known laws of gravity. I've written about that here, but I generally don't mention it. I've learned it's like pissing in the wind. I'm aware you might not believe me but it did happen and to me is one of the very illuminating events of my life. Although there are others. At that time I was in touch with spirit and prayed constantly. I followed what spirit suggested very closely. I know for many reasons, but especially for that, that the world around us isn't real.

I knew in advance of two important relationships coming in, in one other case I told a friend about the person I was going to meet, even his astrological sign, and I met him by chance two hours later. That was quick work.

I've heard a Lady speak in my room in a modulated voice that was separate from myself. She was as real in my room as you would be. She would be an Ascended Spirit but the interesting thing was that she seemed to have her own Agenda, and, yes, she was dispassionate, but she was also there to help me understand that love was important. Perhaps at a greater level of spirit we become dispassionate but retain compassion, helpful but uninvolved. I don't know, perhaps someday we may. Now we see through a glass darkly, as I've mentioned before. Did I mention it too much? I'm sorry. It's a lovely thought and so beautifully worded - and words are important, aren't they?

I've seen in front of me a small golden castle on a hill that wasn't there and failed to see a massive one that was. I was told to get out of London on the morning of 9/11. Nothing happened, but the date is of interest. I was in Gloucester when I heard. I'd followed their instruction. Many things stay in the memory, JFK, Diana, 9/11. They leave their mark on the human psyche.

Today I hear small voices speak to me in the morning, usually succinctly, saying rather dismissive things like "Foolish woman", "You have no idea" (what you've missed) and occasionally favourable and most interesting like "Can you dance with that?" when I've had a good idea or "You'll do". These aren't loud or concerning and I do think they may not be real but they reassure me again that spirit does exist and that sometimes it answers back.

I have an eccentric world view and I'm open to query here as I don't know myself if my ideas are right or wrong and it may be centuries before they're proven one way or the other. For instance, I don't know if the universe exists. It's here I lose any scientists left among my readers. It seems to me we may embellish it as our technology grows and as we reach out so we find wonders that hadn't been there before and I wonder if we're in the process of creating it. Clearly I don't have the vast awareness of a universal creator and the fact is that, despite an interest in the stars or perhaps because of it, I'm still very geo-centric. We may find out some day. Meanwhile, if you're a passionate telescope addict or NASA employee, just keep going because it's all fascinating and beautiful, whether we are creating it as we go or God has put it there and it's endless and expanding, I simply couldn't say, but the wonders there are only now coming into our consciousness and who knows where we're going with that. There are glitches in the matrix sometimes, things that happen that really shouldn't be possible, that should lead us to question some of the realities we're told exist. We manifest into an absolute vacuum where nothing is real, nothing is set and thoughts become things. We can make them wonderful things.

The human mind is powerful. Stay awake to what you're thinking.

44. The Missing Bit to the Law of Abundance End Part

The missing bit is that we live in an unreal world. If we can at all accept that, it will make manifesting our life even easier as nothing around us is real. We live in a world populated by atoms and protons which are in constant flux and movement, which communicate with one another over vast distances and which combine to form the realities we want.

We are great creators, we need only ask and if we ask with belief and with faith and in line with our life's purpose, we receive. This is an immutable law. We visualise and so we become, but we visualise and imagine from an unconscious awareness of who we already are. We are part of spirit.

We manifest into an absolute vacuum where nothing is real, nothing is set and thoughts become things. You can make them great things.

Our visions for ourself and for the world outside us are highly personal. We see in terms of who we are and of what suits us as individuals. If you're a romantic you'll see things in a romanticised way and what you see is subjective. I've said earlier that you don't always see what is around you through the organs of sight, rather you see what the brain compels you to see, and the brain is personalised to an extent. There's really nothing objective about anything I'm saying, what we see, what we aim for, is subjective and if more and more of us aim for a spiritual approach, then that will come into being. Distant healing, for instance, involves hundreds of people and is said to have effect.

In this book I'm attempting to bring together the scientific with the mystical, science which more and more is saying the world is a combination of atoms in flux and the mystical which always says there is a God, there is a universe, there is a compassionate, loving energy somewhere and we are connected to it. At times we feel this through nature (numenism, the belief that spirit inhabits the natural world and natural phenomena), through children, through church, prayer or meditation, but most of us do feel it at some time and in some place or circumstance. More and more, we no longer have a clear dichotomy between the two, the mystical and the scientific, they start to overlap and that is very exciting, as it means, for one thing, that scientists may be less inclined to dismiss the world of the imagination, of the mystical, of the psychic, because most scientists now accept that any of their experiments can be altered by the presence of an observer. This can be a machine, but it can also be a thinking, sentient person whose personal take may alter the outcome of their experiments. That is a development and that is us.

We are creatures of spirit. From spirit we come and to spirit we return. We are loved. We do not know exactly why we are here but we have a feel for our own individual purpose, we know the direction to take and spirit supports our every move in this direction. It may take time and it may take trust, but it will happen. We create into a void, which is important, and our creations take effect. They affect our own life and perhaps that of others. They help us lead a life of joy and fulfilment, which is not as burdensome as it sounds. A life of lightness and fun, with meaning attached. What's not to like? So get going – what's stopping you?

Read everything you can by New Age authors, read the bible, read holy books, read philosophy, and always follow your own instincts and not those of others. Only you can determine your own path and only you and spirit together can bring it to pass.

To end with a quote, I like this one from J.M. Barrie who wrote Peter Pan.

"The reason birds can fly and we can't is simply because they have perfect faith, for to have faith is to have wings."

And I thought it was Red Bull.

The human mind is powerful. Stay awake to what you're thinking.

45. Finally, For Myself

I want again to climb to Grianan of Aileach at dawn and look out over the coasts of Inishowen and hear again the midsummer songs that used to resonate here. I want to hear again harpists and singers in the early morning and see the sun rise over the portacabins (so useful at that time of the morning).

I want to spend time in the North West and see the Atlantic beating against the shore and wild waves carrying surfers inwards towards many beaches at Portrush and Portstewart.

I want to walk the old streets of Derry and cross again the Peace Bridge that divides and unites two different factions. I want at evening time to see the sun set over Derry and Donegal and smell the wild gorse and honeysuckle which flower in Donegal ditches. In my mind I see again wild swans at Inch and I walk again beside the Lake of Shadows where joys and tragedies lurk.

This is what I may do when I am very old and when only memories call.

Maybe I'll see you there.

END

About the Author

2023

The author lives in Northern Ireland and holds an M.A. in languages and a D.F.Astrol.S. from the Faculty of Astrological Studies in London. She has worked as a legal translator, research assistant in psychology, tourist guide and teacher. She's been involved in spirituality and positive thinking from the age of thirteen and is extremely well read on the subject. Drawing from her own many psychic experiences which she writes about here, she has realised that something is missing from the Law of Attraction and that knowledge could help you create your desired life even faster. Originally from Derry in the North West, she returns there when she can and this book is not just a guide to better self-awareness, it is also a memoir of her own life and a hope for the future.

www.ingramcontent.com/pod-product-compliance
Ingram Content Group UK Ltd.
Pitfield, Milton Keynes, MK11 3LW, UK
UKHW022228300325
456897UK00006B/169

9 781967 109654